I0627023

How to Experience the Spiritual Meaning of Gospel Texts:

The Psychology of Reading Mystically

Dr. Loyola Amalraj

Kravitz & Sons

INNOVATORS IN PUBLISHING, MARKETING AND ADVERTISING

Kravitz and Sons LLC
204 E Arlington Blvd. Suite B
Greenville, NC 27858

Published by Kravitz and Sons LLC.

Spirituality and Psychology

ISBN: 979-8-89639-367-2 (sc)
ISBN: 979-8-89639-366-5 (e)

Library of Congress Control Number: 2025918903

Table of Content

Chapter IV

HOW TO EXPERIENCE THE SPIRITUAL MEANING OF GOSPEL TEXTS:
The Psychology of Reading Mystically
Dr. Loyola Amalraj
Ph.D., Marquette University

Contribution to Scholarship:

This study presents a psychological understanding of the prayer exercises of the mystics. It examines the spiritual unconscious, supporting its assertions with clinical evidence. The work asserts how contemplative prayer practices affect brain hemispheres by quieting the left brain and enabling the right brain to journey to the deepest part of consciousness.

From the Foreword:

"This book should serve as an excellent reading not only for Catholic homilists who are seeking fresh insights into liturgical texts but also a practice method for those Christians seeking a new way to meditate on the Scripture."

-Professor Andrew Tomasello
Bauruch College, NY

From a Peer Review:

"...offers a creative and inspiring presentation in his book that integrates sound psychology and spirituality with profound meditations on select gospel texts. A unique feature of this book is that he combines the mystical tradition, methods of meditation and the psychological."

-Dr. Anthony Ciorra
Fordham University,
Bronx, NY

To my beloved parents who inspired me

Foreword

In this volume, Father Loyola Amalraj has put together a study that is at once analytical and metaphysical. Here he presents his interesting insights into how the human mind works in linear and non-linear ways, insights that he has developed over many years of study and service as a priest and teacher. Much of this book exposes his practical application to what is essentially impractical and unstructured, namely, meditation. Not unlike St. Ignatius of Loyola and St. John of the Cross, Father Loyola offers his readers a fairly systematic way to approach an intuitive skill.

In a life assessed from the existentialist point of view, we are "what we do" and not "what we say we do." Similarly, Father Loyola asks us to look beyond the paradox of ritual and faith, to reflect on our own devotion and on our actions, and to find and eliminate the Pharisee in ourselves. He bids us to move to the world of metaphor in our journey to holiness.

In an oft-cited reference, Austrian-born literary theorist Leo Spitzer is said to have pointed out that the cry of the rooster is cock-adoodle-do in English, cocorico in French, kikeriki in German and in Italian. No one would debate which one is correct. Although Father Loyola's roots extend back to the Tamil region of India, this book is very much part of a contemporary American Catholic tradition in that it is at once maps out an interdisciplinary, a multicultural, and a postmodern journey.

This book should serve as an excellent reading not only for Catholic homilists who are seeking fresh insights into liturgical texts but also as a practice method for those Christians seeking a new way to meditate on Scripture. This could be, for some readers, an introduction to meditation. However, Father Loyola's ideas are accessible to those who come from different religious (or even non-religious) backgrounds. He has viewed particular New Testament readings as Christian koans, seeing beyond history, beyond traditional Western thinking, beyond meaning into the obscurity of the God of mystical love.

Feast of St. Joseph of Cupertino, 2009
Dr. Andrew Tomasello
Associate Professor and Deputy Chair for Music
Baruch College Department of Fine Arts and
The Graduate Center (CUNY)

Preface

When I entered a minor seminary in India many years ago, I was very anxious to learn about deep spirituality and make progress in my love for God. It was a very good environment to learn languages such as Latin and English. There were scripture studies, music, and catechism. Sports were required and physical fitness was an integral part of the seminary program. Prayer, meditation, and retreats were an essential part of the training. I remember sitting through morning meditation every day for about a half hour trying to focus on whatever was read aloud slowly and at intervals. This exercise was discursive. Often, I had to fight off falling asleep. Morning, noon, evening, and night prayers were routine. Grand silence followed night prayer. Spiritual conferences were frequently held, almost weekly. All of these activities were to enhance my prayer life later when I became a priest and had to live my life alone in a parish setting.

My studies in the major seminary were extensive in philosophy and systematic theology. Intensive learning was required before I was ready for the day of ordination. The academics helped me considerably for my intellectual life: knowing the correct answer to a theological or philosophical question and rules of canon law. What I found lacking was a serious training in and experience of deep spiritual exercises. Meditation and prayer were explained, and I gained a reasonable understanding and practice of them. Even though I tried to practice and pray I had difficulty not because I did not like them but because there was a lack of intrinsic appeal toward them. The formation, I must admit, was considerably cerebral. Meditation and prayer were frequently forced activities later in my life as a priest. The training nudged me to fulfill obligations of prayer as I promised at my ordination.

Later, graduate studies in secular counseling in the US did not incorporate spiritual methods. I was challenged to bridge a gap between counseling and the spirituality of the mystics. Through the lens of psychology, I was able to understand religious/mystical spirituality. No matter what counseling strategies one employs, without spiritual development, growth in life will remain incomplete. Once an inner transformation occurs by following spiritual practices, human growth can become fully actualized. Deeply spiritual persons are radiant with calm, inner life. What mesmerized me was my mother's natural desire to pray ardently and regularly. I witnessed how praying made her calm and relaxed. Every morning and night I used to wake up and go to bed seeing her so lost in prayer. How did she achieve such a deep, devout experience of prayer? Was it a gift or a result of effort? For years I thought it must have been a special blessing from God for chosen people, but my opinion changed when I started investigating the spiritual exercises of the mystics and experimenting with them myself. It was as if there were a tremendous awakening in me as a result of persisting in the prayer practices.

Consequently, I was able to experience a calm and relaxation that surpassed any sensual experience or pleasure. I also learned that contemplative prayer required persistent effort initially, but once it transported you to a deeper level it then became totally effortless. Repetition of words and phrases that would have otherwise caused monotony and boredom began to still me. My understanding of relaxation changed dramatically. Remaining mindless, effortless in body, and indulging in sensual pleasures are usually understood as relaxation. What I did not know then was that it was only a gateway to something deeper. Simply remaining effortless led to physical, emotional, and intellectual relaxation but it was not the end. Once the mind and body began to become focused, a deep interior focus/concentration started to emerge. In that stage all initial efforts faded away. You experienced something that was already in you but that you did not seek or know before. When I experienced this state of being, it was like feeling at home. Everything after that was effortless and freely given. I just had to hold on to it. I simply received what was freely given to me. I did not feel like letting go of it. This has created in me a natural, spontaneous, intrinsic fervor for prayer and meditation.

This manner of praying has invigorated my prayer life. Rather than being a forced, involuntary activity, it has begun to appeal to me. It started turning out to be my hobby. Willingly, I now get up early in the morning to pray because praying has become a reward in itself. Prayer can also become an experience of deep love. To pray now for me is to love and to love is to pray. Anything can become a reward in itself by the very performance of it rather than hoping for extrinsic pay-back after an action has been completed.

I truly believe the prayer exercises of the mystics can enable any practitioner to experience the deepest love that is beyond relaxation. The physical and emotional effects of spiritual exercises can be affectively experienced by anyone who is willing to practice them. Let what transformed me become contagious! Read, exercise, calm down, and relax.

Rev. Loyola Amalraj, PhD

November, 2025

Email: loyolaamalraj@hotmail.com

Acknowledgments

There has been a voice within me gently prodding me to write down inspirations resulting out of my reflections on daily and Sunday scriptures. Homily preparations, preceded by hours of daily meditation, enable me to think not with my mind but with my heart. Even a day or two after I preach unusual inspirations well up, making me write them down after my homily. Thanks go to the nudging of the Holy Spirit, who was instrumental in the writing of my second book. Reflections were admirable and at times mesmerizing because after hours of praying they were spontaneous and effortless.

Prof. Andrew Tomasello, a medieval musicologist at Baruch College and The Graduate Center (CUNY) and a parishioner, has been one of my best critics. He also has been kind enough to endorse my writing with a foreword. In his own search for contemplative spirituality, he was appreciative of my doctoral dissertation on mental imagery from religious and mystical traditions published my Mellen Press in 2002. Having seen the depth of research that had gone into my first book, he eagerly encouraged me to apply as an adjunct professor to teach a course based on that first published study. I appreciate the interest and enthusiasm he manifested in not only writing a thoughtful foreword but also proofreading my manuscript and making invaluable suggestions.

Dr. Anthony Ciorra, dean of the Graduate School of Religion and Religious Education, Fordham University, New York, first introduced me to Fr. Johnston's classic Mystical Theology: The Science of Love. This book enabled me to investigate the psychology of mysticism, a newly emerging subject, after I had finished teaching a graduate course in Fordham University using my book as the text. Thank you so much for the introduction to the book and immediate response to review the manuscript willingly in the midst of your summer travels and engagements.

I owe my immense gratitude to two of my doctoral panel members, Dr. Mark Kipfmueller and Dr. John Johnson, who have been reviewing scholars of my manuscript on behalf of Mellen Press for its publicity. Since my graduation from Marquette University, Milwaukee, Wisconsin, they have been in constant touch with me encouraging me to contribute further to the subject matter I undertook to investigate in my research and expressing their hope to read my next book. Thanks to your persistent inspiration and the gracious reviews.

I have a team of personal friends from various fields who offered to proofread my manuscript: David Andros, Gail Anshus, Mary Dibb, Richard Fuerst, Marjorie Gilbert, Sr. Mary Hertrich, Kathy Olszewski, Olive Wallace, Judee Weber, and William Wojnar, Jr. Marjorie Gilbert volunteered graciously to help out with checking the Bible quotes and indexing besides proofreading and David Ciasca assisted me readily with manuscript typesetting. Many thanks for their tireless support of my work. Painstakingly, they all went through the manuscript and made suggestions and corrections. My thanks to every one of them for the job so generously done.

Frank Burrows was my editor-in-chief. Without his persistent hard work and literary criticism, this work would not have seen the light of day. His offer to edit this manuscript from start to finish has been amazing. His sincerity of heart and professional application to the job with his background as an English teacher was as much a learning experience as the inspiration from the books I examined for the research topic. He had the patience to analyze each and every word in a sentence and suggested ways of reconstructing them without discarding my original words. Without his gracious, generous, dedicated, and ever obliging heart and endearing responses, I would not have been able to make this kind of progress in the manuscript. I offer him my sincere thanks from the bottom of my heart. Sr. Johnalyn Witkowski, SSND, was phenomenal in her final proofreading of my second manuscript as she did with my first. Indeed, she did a professional job and I thank the gentle soul for the excellent work.

I would like to acknowledge my sincere gratitude to the publisher Kravitz and Sons for seeking me out for republication. Lily Ross the author advisor shared with me how their professional reviewers which included her, found my work worthwhile to be republished under their genre of inspirational books. In addition, I was told over 45 bookstores across the country expressed an interest in putting out the book on their book shelves for sales. It is incredible that they did take a survey to get feedback before contacting me with this prospect. This I believe is providential both for the selecting reviewers as well as the author. For them to dig through material published fifteen years ago and desire to bring it to light speaks volumes. I believe the reviewers themselves are set on a mission to search for truth. After a serious process of discernment they choose the authors. Just as they were affected by what they had read in my work, I hope, my readers too would take time to read my work slowly in small groups or individually, question, wonder, discuss, discern, debate and practice what is relevant, meaningful and practical. It would enable them to journey within to discover the ever present and endearing Presence that simply accepts and embraces each of us as we are unconditionally. Such an encounter I believe will alter the center of gravity in each one.

I gratefully acknowledge many friends and individuals who resonated with the message through the homilies and presentations. Your affirmation is a validation of my contemplative silence that nurtures me when I pray hours long, prepare and share.

Transformation is something you cannot pretend to have if you did not experience it; nor could hide it if you had been transformed. My response to the prospect of republication was never motivated by monitory profit, but it is to altruistically share the joy that is indwelling, with each of you.

Rev. Loyola Amalraj, PhD

Mukwonago, Wisconsin

Email: loyolaamalraj@hotmail.com

Introduction

When I enrolled in a graduate program in counseling at Marquette University in Milwaukee, Wisconsin, I hoped to learn skills that would enable me to understand my own problems and handle them better. I desired also to help others in the same way. The reason I chose counseling as my major was to analyze secular ways to understand how psychological methods can be understood and applied more effectively to spirituality. Christian spiritual exercises are founded on theological and doctrinal beliefs. These exercises may be dry and abstract rather than personal and deeply engaging. What I did not understand then was that both the psychological and the spiritual could be complementary. Or, further, that the psychological was incomplete without the spiritual, and the spiritual was not as easily applicable to human conditions without an understanding of the psychological.

Unfortunately, my years spent studying counseling did not find much bridge-building between these two branches. Therefore, I desired to combine psychological methods with the deeply spiritual exercises of the mystics. Coincidentally, this combination led to a deeper reflection on and grasp of the scriptures that I read and reflect on for daily liturgy. Illustrating how spiritual exercises effect psychological, biological, and neurological transformation is the primary component and motivation of this book. The second aim of the book is to examine how the mind can transcend itself influenced by contemplative prayer to let the spirit simply receive inspirational messages for the heart from scriptures. Many small reflections on gospel passages are presented as samples for inspiration resulting out of prayer practices.

There is a strong desire for deeper spirituality now more than even a decade ago. While fervor for profound holiness persists, efforts to be religious in the traditional sense have waned. In other words, people seem somewhat less enthusiastic about religious worship. In its place, a longing for personal spirituality has intensified. Institutions that conduct worship and rituals have been challenged to satisfy this newly emerging interest. When people find their quest for personal spirituality unaddressed within their own church they move on to another church. Sometimes they seek spiritual methods from religious traditions other than the one to which they had been committed or in which they have had their upbringing. What is clearly emerging is an insatiable need for deep spirituality. Religions across the world, particularly Christian churches, are being forced to reexamine their traditional ways and do some soul searching. Otherwise, their adherents are likely to find other ways to satisfy their desire for deeper spirituality.

Traditional churches maintain places of worship. Believers gather together daily or weekly to celebrate the word and/or sacraments. The Catholic Church celebrates the breaking of bread and word daily. Homilies are incorporated into the celebration. Other denominations center on proclamation of the word primarily, without sacramental celebrations. In both settings opportunity for communal worship is provided. What is found missing though, is a personal spirituality that enables believers to engage more wholeheartedly in the communal worship. Mere repetition of an external ritual may be impersonal, empty, and mechanical. Attendance at an evangelical preaching and gathering may lack the tangibility of sacraments which intensifies faith. A communal gathering provides an opportunity to enter into the mystery of celebration, but the individual may still feel disconnected. Communal services may appeal merely to reason and simply promote intellectual ways of participation. The heart of the individual may not tune into the celebration if it is not trained in private prayer and meditation. Whatever the individual is performing or whatever is being performed collectively by the congregation has to be absorbed individually. Otherwise, it will surely lead to frustration.

Communal worship may not necessarily gain the attention of the individual unless the person has been trained to establish a personal relationship with God. Private prayer and devotion have to be promoted. One of the best ways to enable believers to participate in the liturgy enthusiastically is to show them how to pray and meditate effectively. What is needed is not a mere rational explanation or definition of how to pray or simply a laying down of the rules just as it used to be said: pray, pay, and obey. That kind of prayer involves reason and intellect. But the body and its emotions can and should also become integral parts of prayer. Use of the senses and imagination of sensations can make meditation more effective. Preceded by deep meditative exercises, personal vocal/mental prayer can lead to a state beyond relaxation. After all, such practices have long existed in the traditions of the Church. Somehow they have been neglected or sidelined because it is possible that we have become cerebral and doctrinal in practicing our faith. Today modern science and psychology are fascinated by the impact of meditation on physiology (Borysenko, 1987). How repetitive prayers and methods of meditation can literally slow down mechanisms of the body is being studied in laboratories (Benson, 1996). The measurable impact of spiritual exercises on body and mind is being investigated in clinical studies. Often, they can enhance a cerebral practice of faith and make it tangibly experiential.

There is a growing need to understand the potential of effective prayer methods from a clinical perspective. Traditional contemplative prayers are being tested and shown to be effective. Monastic prayer methods have been brought out of the monastery for experimental purposes. People are inquisitive about different methods of prayer that are usually associated with religious and monastic communities. Clinical evidence demonstrates that people can experience deeper relaxation while praying (Benson, 1984). It offers credence to the efficacy of prayer. Together with mandatory communal celebrations based on doctrine and tradition, personal experience, gained through the practice of meditative exercises, can lead to fulfilling and going beyond the requirements of institutionalized religions. External obligations cannot be passively and ritually carried out without interior transformation.

In this book the author will attempt to unlock the secrets of contemplative prayer methods that will contribute to a personal desire for prayer and worship. The book will incorporate medical and clinical evidence supporting the efficacy of prayer. How a prolonged practice of contemplative prayer can enable one to grasp deeper levels of meanings in the scriptures will be explained. Earnest practice of contemplative prayer transforms one beyond relaxation to experience pure consciousness beneath thinking and feeling. Once someone becomes present to the indwelling presence of God, the heart will begin slowly to know the unknown. The individual will begin to speak a paradoxical language because the person will see the unseen. Such a presence cannot be grasped intellectually but can only be experienced in the heart.

The first chapter will present a background for a deeper understanding of the scriptures. Scriptures can be analyzed in multiple ways: theologically, philosophically, sociologically, and/or historically to name a few. These perspectives may contain abstractions or concepts not easily applicable to the individual and modern society. When scripture is viewed from a psychological perspective, personal implications may be more apparent to the individual and may rather be found relevant and even interesting. Psychology is a study of the mind. Without an understanding of the soul and God any psychological journey is incomplete. The spiritual component of an individual is as and more important than physical and psychological aspects. This section will examine how contemplative prayer, both vocal and mental, can contribute to a deep meditative state as opposed to cerebral or discursive prayer. Clinical evidence from medical science concerning the effects of meditation on the brain and nervous system will be presented.

The second chapter will explain how medical science and psychology add to the understanding of the impact of the spiritual exercises on body and mind. Although for nearly two centuries psychology has generally dissociated itself from the study of religion, within the past two decades, a newly emerging movement known as "transpersonal psychology" has investigated how spiritual disciplines impact mind, body, and spirit. Humans are incomplete by themselves and are only parts of the Whole. With the explosion of psychological studies in the past century it is necessary to translate Biblical ideas to incorporate psychological concepts and enable people to personalize them in practical ways.

How people journey from the conscious mind to the unconscious to the spiritual unconscious levels of being will be examined from the perspective of transpersonal psychology. This chapter will demonstrate how research on contemplative prayer reveals that there is an intrinsic connection between concentration and relaxation. Generally in our experience, concentration and relaxation are polarized: one excludes the other. But concentration through meditation leads eventually to deep relaxation and even beyond toward the unknown indwelling presence of the Absolute.

In the third chapter the author will present different levels of meanings in the scriptures. Mystics, who practice contemplative prayer methods, reflect on the scriptures and material realities differently and make paradoxical statements. Practice of their methods can empower modern believers to connect to deeper meanings in the scriptures and the revelation can lead to greater conviction. Different stages or levels of prayer lead to a gradually growing union with God. Training mind, body, and spirit with these types of prayers will allow people to experience calming of the mind and relaxation of the body, in turn making their communal worship meaningful, relevant, and personal. Samples of prayer methods of great mystics and their contemplative prayer practices will be briefly examined to show how senses of the body and the imagination of its sensations can be engaged by the intellect to journey beyond rationality.

The fourth chapter will offer samples of mystical reflections on gospel passages. Psychological inquiry can be employed to examine and understand how to practice the methods of contemplatives. Mystics and their prayer methods have been analyzed mostly from a theological perspective. A psychological understanding of the spirituality of the mystics will show how individuals today can imitate the prayer methods of the mystics and enjoy their impact on body, mind, and spirit. Persevering in contemplative prayer methods as understood from a psychological perspective then leads one to greater understanding of the psychological implications contained in the scriptures. Fully immersed in the psychological meanings, the individual can become open to radical changes resulting from a personal sense of contemplative prayer practices. Further, the individual is better prepared for transformation of consciousness, the goal of personal/communal spiritual exercises. As a matter of fact, worshipers can live untransformed lives and believe that they love God and hope to gain heaven later in the life-after through performances of good deeds on earth without caring to receive the Kingdom that comes to us as a free gift here and now. Inspired by the words of scripture, realities of the world may subsequently seem paradoxical, reversing our vision of reality and seeing it from God's perspective. Like Paul, one can experience the power of God even in one's weakness and sinfulness.

Chapter I

Definitions

It is important that I define the topic chosen for the book. The book is partly entitled The Psychology of Reading Mystically. This seems like an unusual topic. What do I mean by that? Five years ago I happened to come across a book, entitled Mystical Theology: the Science of Love by William Johnston, S.J. (1995). What fascinated me was that Johnston had gone to great lengths to describe mysticism. Messages from this book are what my heart had been yearning for years to hear. This book is about how one can be internally and externally transformed by a mystical union with God here on Earth. Johnston's book encompasses methods mainly from Christian traditions, but he has also correlated his findings with other traditions such as Buddhism and Hinduism. He describes the theological journey of the Christian mystics so well that it is indeed a classic. What I find complementary to his work is the deep understanding that results from an examination of the prayer methods of the mystics from a psychological standpoint. In order to accomplish that, I will be examining the scriptures from a psychological as opposed to a theological perspective. This will enable readers to apply this new perspective directly to their own psychological states drawing meaning for their personal lives rather than knowing them simply from a theological or doctrinal point of view. Both perspectives are interconnected, but I am attempting to highlight the psychological perspective. Maintaining a balance between theological and psychological interpretation is like performing a delicate dance.

The contemplative prayer methods of the mystics can be examined from a psychological point of view, keeping in mind their theological background. A theological analysis of their methods will convey different meanings as opposed to a psychological understanding. Psychological ways of examining the methods will teach readers how to understand and practice them directly in their lives without ignoring their theological foundations. A psychological understanding of the scriptures and contemplative prayers provides one with an appreciation of the richness of gospel passages. The author proposes that perseverance in practice of the prayer methods of the mystics enables one to grasp deeper layers of meanings contained in the scriptures. Insights can be very paradoxical. That is why most of the samples of gospel reflections that follow in the fourth chapter contain topics that are paradoxical in nature.

More than likely the words "mystical," "mysticism," and "mystic" are quite apt to be misunderstood. The word mystical as an adjective may allude to mysteries that are unlikely to be easily understood by humans. It may refer to belonging or adhering to esoteric or secret rites, doctrines, or practices. It may mean something beyond human comprehension or something that is enigmatic or that which fills one with wonder and awe. It implies magical power. Mystical may also refer to some obscure or occult character or meaning such as mystical powers as in Webster's dictionary (1988). The same dictionary defines mysticism as 1) "the doctrines or beliefs of mysteries; specifically, the doctrine that it is possible to achieve communion with God through contemplation; and 2) any doctrine that asserts the possibility of attaining an intuitive knowledge of spiritual truths through meditation" (p. 898). The definition of a mystic, as partly borrowed from the same dictionary, is an individual who becomes passively receptive to communion with God and is blessed with an intuitive knowledge of spiritual truths through perseverance in loving practices of meditation and contemplation. From this flows an understanding of the words mystical and mysticism.

Psychological Understanding of the Scriptures

Scripture passages can be understood from multiple perspectives such as theological, philosophical, or historical. Each perspective has its own goal. The objective of all is to impart some meaning to humanity so that they may provide some guidelines and direction. In the past century, psychology has made strides in the understanding of the human psyche. Dynamics that arise from the interactions of mind and body have been clarified by four major theories: psychoanalytic, behavioral, humanistic, and transpersonal. Within the last decade the fourth force in psychology, known as transpersonal or psychospiritual theory, has investigated the impact of the relationship between the spirit and the Absolute. This theory has provided opportunities to analyze how the practice of spiritual exercises from various traditions has measurable physiological and psychological effects on the individual.

Recognizing how much the Western world has been influenced by psychology, Keating (1994) introduces the term "Divine Therapy" in his book, Intimacy with God (p. 72). In the presence of the Divine Therapist Jesus Christ, one's psyche not only recognizes its illness but also drops its defenses. Many are unaware of how sick they are. Even to identify our sinfulness we need assistance from God. In the divine relationship humans can develop friendship as well as healing. "Reading the gospel from the perspective of contemporary psychotherapy provides us with a detailed diagnosis of the disease" notes Keating (1994, p. 74). Many of the biblical stories, parables, psalms, and sayings portray the ongoing human drama that is being staged in our daily lives. Looking at them through a psychological lens we can better understand our lives. God's word is eternal in this sense. The past is made alive right now even though the sacred scriptures were written about two millennia ago.

Religious practices affect people psychologically. Medical studies are being conducted on how religious factors have a profound influence on people. Studies record how religious practitioners experience higher levels of survival; reduced addictive habits such as alcoholism, drug abuse, and smoking; decreased anxiety, depression, and anger; reduced blood pressure; and improvement in conditions such as cancer and heart diseases. Psychology and medical science study these impacts seriously. Physical and mental states such as anger, depression, anxiety and other abnormalities are being investigated thoroughly by psychology (Beary & Benson referenced in Samuels & Samuels, 1975).

Understanding scripture from a psychological perspective is essential because it can then be better applied to the human condition. If a person suffering from anger, depression, or anxiety can reflect on the Word of God, it will speak to that individual's personal condition. Christian counselors use the message of the Bible to gain leverage with their clients if he/she is a practicing Christian. Many theories of Christian counseling and spiritual direction explore the possibility of bringing a scriptural understanding into the field of counseling. The more the connections are created the greater will be the increase of healing and faith in God.

Let me present an example of how to understand scripture by commenting on a passage theologically. Then, by focusing on the psychological perspective, I will demonstrate how one can absorb it in such a way that it becomes applicable to the mental and the emotional state of the individual. In Luke's Acts of the Apostles, the Council of Jerusalem is convened to address the issue of circumcision of the Gentiles as demanded by certain Jewish Christians (Acts 15: 1-29). Together with the elders of the community, the apostles discuss the issue. Peter reveals how God calls the Gentiles to faith by pouring the Holy Spirit upon them (15: 6-12). After much debate and prayer James, the leader of the Jerusalem community, reflecting the thoughts of those who participated, instructs that the Gentiles be exempted from circumcision, but that they "avoid pollution from idols, unlawful marriage, the meat of the strangled animals, and blood" (15: 20). From a theological perspective we can see how the apostles arrived at this difficult conclusion that God's call to faith was universal by not making circumcision mandatory. The Council agrees with Paul's and Barnabas' plea after much discussion and reflection. Through them the Council sends a letter to the Gentile communities in Antioch, Syria, and Cilicia (Acts 15: 23-29). The Council was guided by the Holy Spirit to take a daring stand as a fledgling community against the voice of tradition.

From a psychological perspective, we can conclude that rules mandated by religions regarding spirituality will have to be substituted by the love of God and neighbor. Rules and laws are only the minimum. By merely fulfilling them externally, correctly, and exactly, we may not and need not be totally transformed. Deep in the heart one can still remain unaffected by external performances. That is where Paul inspires us by distinguishing between the letter of the law and the spirit of the law. Faith in Jesus requires a deep personal relationship as opposed to being merely law abiding, focusing on external requirements. When an individual personalizes his/her relationship with God it becomes possible to multiply the rules whereby one is actually freed from laws. A burdensome following of rules can be made intrinsically attractive if the individual learns how to personalize the laws of religion. When we combine this psychological understanding with the theological in the above-mentioned section concerning the decision of the Jerusalem Council, it can be reflected upon much differently. Once this new understanding occurs, no one needs to tell the believer why and how to follow rules. Mere uninternalized, correct, and exact observance of rules cannot lead to ultimate fulfillment, transformation. When the believer understands that it is not so much about doing it right as making the practice personal, then the individual will seek more than simply fulfilling duties. A theological understanding may be limited to the confines of rational knowledge alone without permeating the whole person. Mind and body become fully engaged in the journey of the soul toward the Absolute if the person enjoys an inner experience of God as opposed to mere unengaging adherence to external obligations.

Mystics' Ways of Understanding the Scriptures

An examination of the mystics' prayer methods reveals that their exercises are rooted in the scriptures. Further we can see how different contemplative prayer methods in fact enhance their understanding of scripture passages (Acts 15: 23-29). In their practice of methods and understanding of the scripture there is a relationship of mutuality. Allow me to demonstrate with an analogy. From the standpoint of a contemplative, the passage of the blind man Bartimaeus (Mk 10: 46-52) can be read very slowly two or three times. A simple reflection can then follow. After a brief analysis of the subject matter in the mind, one could move from thinking about it to affectation. How? Connect with feelings that would arise in you if you were the blind man. You could gradually move beyond the emotions related to desire for healing from your own blindness. How?

Sit comfortably and close your eyes. Whatever word(s), phrase(s), or a sentence such as "heal me, help me, touch me," etc., resonate with you, repeat them slowly as a mantra or focus word(s) first vocally for some time and later mentally, in your heart. You may synchronize them with your heartbeat and recite them rhythmically. Prolonged, gentle repetition gradually will transcend reasoning, analyzing, and evaluating the theological significance, as well as the accompanying emotions, and will move you towards an unknowing, calm, and fulfilling inner experience. Rational knowledge at this stage becomes a personally transformative experience. It will be more effective than a simple intellectual understanding or emotional experience. If a person persists in this sort of practice it will lead to enlightenment deep inside without having to indulge in rational analyses or emotional examinations. Healing is experienced once contact is made with the unfailing, indwelling presence of God. The soul, regardless of physical, emotional, or intellectual wounds, is healed by union with the Absolute in love. Spiritual healing completes the healing in this union.

Mystics make use of reason also to understand. So we do need an intellectual understanding to facilitate an appreciation of deeper meanings. Despite our best efforts to grasp meaning there will be matters beyond our intellectual understanding. As humans, we are not able to deal with mystery fully from the standpoint of reason alone. Let us look at some theological mysteries: the Incarnation, Immaculate Conception, presence of Jesus in the Eucharist, and Holy Trinity to name a few. The human mind can have only partial understanding of these mysteries.

Theologically, they can be explained to some degree. Psychologically, it is even harder to fathom them. So our analysis of these mysteries comes to a grinding halt at some point. We will be called upon to have faith in God not only with our understanding but even without it. Believers will be beckoned to worship God through "unknowing" as well as knowing. This is where mystics lend us a helping hand. The Cloud of Unknowing (Walsh, 1981), a fourteenth century classic, illustrates this notion beautifully. According to this work, the soul is wedged between two clouds: one above, known as the cloud of unknowing, between itself and God and one below, known as the cloud of forgetting, between itself and God's creatures. On one hand the soul has to love what cannot be known and on the other it has to disregard what it finds to be tangibly real.

Mystics believe that there are different levels and degrees of meaning contained in the scriptures. By reflection some of them can be grasped. The more one knows, the more one is still in need of understanding deeper layers of meaning. Huston Smith, a scholar of world religions, reports that the Sufis, mystics of Islam, believe each verse in the Koran, the holy book of Islam, has seven to seventy hidden layers of meaning (1991). Knowledge may help one grasp a few, but the rest will have to be simply revealed. The key for such revelation is not an intellectual process but sheer repetition of some verses in the heart. Most transformative understanding is freely granted for persevering in faith-filled and heartfelt repetition as opposed to attempting to reason out the meanings of verses. For an untrained person this is intriguing because repetition of mantras, or words and verses, usually leads to boredom. But the contemplative uses repetition merely to be receptive to divine revelation. While an unschooled person may be bored by the monotony, the mystic finds it exciting because the same looks new every time it is recited. There is a deep physiological, psychological, sentimental, and spiritual journey embedded in the invocation. It leads to a place which is beneath or above thinking and feeling. It transports one to the soul where God is ever-present. It moves one away from being self-conscious to an experience of Pure Consciousness as many religions such as Hinduism describe. It is an experience of pure being where the human self unites with the divine Self, finding its completeness, fullness, and the "image" and "likeness" of God (Gen 1: 26).

Dr. Deepak Chopra (1989), an endocrinologist and renowned author who lectures internationally, divides the subjective state of awareness according to ancient Indian psychology into three phrases: waking, sleeping, and dreaming. The same reality assumes different levels of being in different states of consciousness. A wild animal in a dream state is different from an animal in a waking state. "It obeys entirely different laws, and similarly, the laws of the sleep state, although not known to the conscious mind, must be distinct from those of the waking and dreaming states" (Chopra, p. 169). Indian mystics postulate the existence of a fourth state of awareness known as the "beyond state," which transcends the three normal states of experience. The ability to access this fourth state does not result from "thinking" but the phenomenon is "immediate, nonverbal, and...totally transforming" (p. 170). Usually, the doorway to this stage lies between being awake and falling asleep.

Chopra further substantiates his thesis by examining the work of an American psychologist, Robert Keith Wallace. In 1967, Wallace investigated the physiological changes of Transcendental Meditation (which uses the repetition of a syllable to experience calming of the mind). In his study, Wallace was able to quantify how during meditation physiological changes resulted in lowered heart rate and blood pressure, an increase in the radiation of alpha waves from the brain, decreased oxygen consumption, and other measurable changes. The meditators were able to reach a calming state within a few minutes of meditation compared to similar relaxation a person experiences only after four to six hours of sleep. They experienced "absolute inner silence, a feeling of vast expansion, and a profound knowing....The mind was emptied of all specific thoughts but was left with the clear awareness of 'I know everything'" (Chopra, 1989, p. 176). There was evidence of deep knowing in their unknowing in the fourth state of awareness. Clinical studies explain why mystics as practitioners of meditation constantly indulge in vocal or mental repetitions of syllables, words, or phrases. Transportation to a higher consciousness is made possible by drumming the conscious mind ceaselessly with repetition. A focused mind leads to focused awareness of the moment, a small taste of timelessness, eternity.

Secrets of Mystical Life

Mystic is derived from the Greek word myein which means "to shut the eyes." It is something that is mysterious and cannot be solely grasped by the intellectual pursuit. It is a "spiritual experience that depends upon neither sensual nor rational methods; but it is the inner light which arises from the wisdom of the heart" (Schimmel, 1975 quoted in Amalraj 2002, p. 269). Inge (1948) defines a mystic as "someone who has been, or is being initiated into some esoteric knowledge of Divine things, about which he must keep his mouth shut" (quoted in Amalraj, 2002, p. 197). Mysticism itself is defined as "the attempt to realize, in thought and feeling, the immanence of the temporal in the eternal, and of the eternal in the temporal" (Inge, 1948, p. 5). Mystical life itself is seen as an experience of the revelation of divine secrets, divine life. It is a knowing that cannot be clearly expressed in words because it is beyond the description of words or the expression of concepts.

Different Forms or Stages of Prayer:

Generally, we can distinguish three methods or stages: prayer, meditation, and contemplation. Although they are separate activities, the term prayer can be applied to all three because they are all forms of prayer. What is prayer? Prayer in general can be understood as raising our hearts and minds to God. It is "the raising of one's mind and heart to God or the requesting of good things from God" (John Damascene, quoted in Catechism of the Catholic Church, Libreria Editrice Vaticana, 1994, p. 613). It is pouring out to God whatever thoughts and emotions occur to us as they arise. "For me, prayer is a surge of the heart; it is a simple look turned toward heaven, it is a cry of recognition and of love, embracing both trial and joy" (St. Therese of Lisieux, quoted in Catechism of the Catholic Church, Libreria Editrice Vaticana, 1994, p. 613).

Prayer in General

We may consider two forms of prayer: spontaneous and canonical. Spontaneous prayer is not limited to any place, time, form, or manner. Anyone can pray at any time for anything in any way. It may be as short as a word; a sentence said once or repeated; or as lengthy as a prolonged monologue. It may be further classified as prayer of praising, thanksgiving, repentance, petition, intercession, blessing, adoration, and so on. As the nomenclature of these categories suggests, their purposes are explicit in their names. The second form of prayer is canonical. This is the official prayer of the Church consisting of psalms, scriptures, and the spiritual writings of saints recited daily by ordained ministers, consecrated religious, and the laity. These prayers are specific to different times of the day such as morning, noon, evening, and night and different seasons of the year following the Church calendar such as Advent, Christmas, Lent, Easter, and Ordinary Time. The consecrated faithfully recite them either individually or collectively at certain times by requirement of Church law by virtue of their consecration or ordination. For the laity it is optional. Many pray them devoutly every day just as the religious or ordained. Another aspect of this prayer is that it can be vocal or mental. Commonly, it is vocal when a community prays aloud or sings it but it could be mental when prayed silently by an individual or group. This exercise may be examined as another form called silent or loud prayer. It depends on how a prayer is performed: Is it prayed out loud or silently within? Both types have a transformative effect.

One of the disadvantages of canonical prayer is that it may not always be as engaging in a fully devotional manner as it should be. There is no way of gauging whether or not this prayer is responded to other than simply reading the signs of what transpires after the prayer. Although all prayers are heard by God, we may very well be granted favors without prayer. Only the heart of the individual can measure whether or not praying in itself brings about an effect physically and emotionally. It is not just the result of prayer alone that we need to watch for but what effect the prayer itself and the manner of praying has on the individual. Another disadvantage of canonical prayer is when it is performed as an obligation or duty without personalizing it. It can be a mere mechanical activity or performance when recited collectively because most often other activities either precede or follow it.

Within a community it is usually done within a certain time frame and speed. Unless effort is made by the individual and community to recite these prayers meditatively they may be unaffecting. Because this form of prayer may be performed under mandate it may not personally affect the individual so as to experience a calming of mind and body. It may be exercised as a sort of one more vocal or mental activity. The prayer (one who prays) may be aware of the subject matter from a rational perspective, i.e., being conscious of words and their meanings. Sometimes emotions can well up within the person as prayers are prayed depending on the theme and personal experience. Ideas and emotions can combine with what is being prayed. Yet the deeper part of our being known as the heart, the seat of wisdom, may not be fully involved with the intellectual and emotional activity. For prayer to be effective, focus or concentration of mind is essential. The greater the focus the greater is its impact. The next level is meditation which can enhance the focus of mind, making prayer much more appealing.

Meditative Prayer

The word "meditate" in Webster's dictionary (1988) derives from the Latin word meditari which means to reflect upon, study, ponder; plan or intend; think deeply and continuously, reflect and muse. The word "meditation" derives from meditatio meaning the act of deep, continued thought, solemn reflection on sacred matters as a devotional act; often in plural form: oral or written material, such as a sermon, centered on meditation (p. 842). First and foremost, meditation seeks to engage the mind in a serious thought process as the various definitions indicate. In Catechism of the Catholic Church (1994) meditation is said to be a "quest" which, I believe, is intellectual, emotional, and spiritual (p. 649). We constantly seek to know how God wants us to live our lives. To fix our focus on prayer we may use visuals such as the Bible, particularly the gospels, icons, holy pictures, and great writings on spirituality by saintly men and women. Generally speaking, intellect or reason dominates the process. Using reason we try to discern what God asks of us. Various methods of effective prayer have been expounded by spiritual masters. In short, "meditation engages thought, imagination, emotion, and desire" (p. 650). A combination of all these must play a significant role in this form of prayer.

In his lengthy introduction to the Spiritual Exercises of St. Ignatius, Ganss (1991) distinguishes three stages in spiritual theology: 1) discursive mental prayer, 2) affective mental prayer, and 3) contemplative mental prayer.

Discursive Mental Prayer

Discursive prayer consists primarily of "multiple acts of reasoning" even though emotions are in part implied in it. A great deal of intellectual discussion, pleas, conversation, and negotiation occur in our dialogue with God. Thoughts are mixed with emotions, and there is a tremendous sense of awareness of sinfulness or unholiness in the individual. Traditionally, this prayer is called the "purgative way" or "stage" of growth in the spiritual path. Generally, this is appropriate for beginners (Ganss, 1991, p. 62). Recognizing the immeasurable contrast between the Infinite Self and the self, the initiate indulges in "contrition, confession, and hearty amendment" (Inge, 1948, p. 10). Through a journey of discipline and mortification, purgation brings about a "state of pain and effort" (Underhill, 1990, p. 169). Bodily and intellectual activities abound in the first ladder of the mystical life.

Affective Mental Prayer

In affective mental prayer the human faculties of "will, intellect, and feeling" are centered on God (Inge, 1948, p. 11). Affectations or emotions predominantly characterize this second stage of prayer, traditionally known as the "illuminative way." Specifically, it centers on love. Love and passion may dwell in the heart of the one seeking this path or who is at this stage. The welling up of emotions is orchestrated by the intellect, but the emotions tend to dominate. Reason is diminished in importance. Passionate feelings such as gratitude, joy, admiration, mercy, forgiveness, providence, protection, and the like are spontaneously felt and expressed in thoughts and words as they are experienced. The intellect may listen, experience, and express the flow of affects as they are perceived.

Contemplative Mental Prayer

In this form of prayer various activities are simplified in a loving gaze upon God. This is exercised by those who are advanced and developed spiritually. It is known as the "unitive way." This brings the meditator into a loving union with God. Constant communication brings about an interior union with God which then flows into one's actions. This is where the mystical union occurs. The soul is united to the Absolute.

In the Christian tradition there are two types of contemplation: acquired versus infused or active versus passive. In the former, human industry is necessary in the beginning stage but nevertheless the outcome does not result from human efforts but is rather a pure gift from God. Human effort is assisted by divine grace and transformation is the end result. In the latter stage, prayer becomes "supernatural" which means no human activity is necessary because it is entirely God's work in the soul. St. Teresa of Avila compares the former to the water flowing from a distant source into the trough whereas in the latter it is like a spring that bubbles up (Kavanaugh & Rodriguez, 1979).

Chapter II

Studies by Medical Science and Transpersonal Psychology

Since the 1960s medical science has been investigating the practice of meditation from the perspective of healing physical and psychological conditions. Physicians treating patients are fascinated by the power of faith in the process of recovery. In addition to clinical assistance from doctors, patients seemed to have used their faith to experience healing. The faith factor has become a matter of interest for medical practitioners who started investigating practices of meditation and prayer that offered relief sometimes in conjunction with and at other times regardless of medical procedures. The pioneer in the field in the late 1960s was Dr. Herbert Benson from Harvard Medical School.

Together with a group of doctors and scientists, Benson set out to investigate the spiritual practices of Tibetan Buddhist monks in the Indian Himalayas. After obtaining permission from the Dalai Lama, his team conducted experiments on monks living in isolated hermitages practicing a particular form of meditation known as Tum-mo yoga. These experiments studied how the monks were able to increase their body temperature so as to be able to warm icy clothes placed on their bodies in the freezing Himalayan climate. Instruments measured the vital signs and body temperature of the monks before, during, and after meditation which lasted for over an hour. The power of mind over body was demonstrated in the monks' ability to raise their body temperatures over 13 degrees Fahrenheit. Reportedly, the monks held a competition among themselves with wet, icy sheets on their bodies during wintry moonlit nights to determine who dried clothes faster or melted the largest amount of ice with their body heat during meditation.

In his later studies Benson was able to discover that meditative techniques were able to produce what he termed the "Relaxation Response" that could be observed in quantifiable physiological changes. The state enables one to attain a "form of mental concentration that distracted individuals from their usual cares and concerns and focused their minds" (Borysenko, 2007, pp. 16-17). Meditation rooted in deep faith of some sort, either in religion or a doctor, contributed significantly to the positive or negative responses of the body. The power of belief in something was revealed to be an asset to the patients who experienced healing. Meditative practices emerging from personal belief made significant differences in healing (Benson, 1984). Later, Benson conducted experiments on practitioners of meditation using a consistent focus word or phrase repeated with closed eyes in a dark room. His studies on meditation noted physiological changes such as low levels of oxygen consumption, decreased heart rate and breathing rate, low blood pressure, and intensification of Alpha brain waves. Based on his findings he concluded that the relaxation response was just the opposite of what he called the "fight-or-flight" response (Benson, 1975, p. 23). He described it as a "hypometabolic state" in which he observed a relaxed performance of the sympathetic nervous system (Samuels & Samuels, 1975).

Wallace researched the physiological changes that took place during Transcendental Meditation (repetition of a mantra) and found results that supported Benson's work (Chopra, 1989). He measured practitioners' brain waves, blood pressure, heart rate, and other physical changes. His subjects reported a state of deep relaxation in which they experienced slower breathing and heart rate, decreased oxygen levels and their EEGs (electroencephalograms) measured increased levels of alpha waves. The subjects also reported feelings of "inner silence, peacefulness, and relaxation" (Chopra, 1989, p. 176). Wallace concluded that his measurements indicated that the state experienced by the subjects was very different from normal waking, dreaming, or sleeping. He postulated a different fourth state of consciousness he called "hypometabolic wakefulness" (Chopra, 1989, p. 176).

Benson proposed an eight step meditation for the Relaxation Response (1984, pp. 106- 117). The following steps incorporate small and succinct additions as variations based on my own research of the contemplative prayer methods of major mystical traditions (Amalraj, 2002).

Step One: Pick up a word or short phrase that is essential to your belief system.

Selecting a word or phrase is very important for the focus or meditation. To achieve the Relaxation Response, evidenced by a reduction of beta waves and an increase of alpha waves in the brain, a decrease in blood flow from the muscles and an increase in blood flow to the brain and skin "producing a feeling of warmth and rested mental alertness" (Borysenko, 2007, p. 17), Benson believes what he calls the "Faith Factor" has to be an integral part of meditation (1984, p. 106).

By Faith Factor he means instead of selecting a neutral word such as "one," or a syllable such as Om, choosing a word or phrase rooted in your belief system performs a two-fold function. It makes the meditation very effective because of the power of belief and it also enhances one's faith through an exercise of it in its simplest form. From a physiological perspective the practice decreases anxiety and it is effective in treating a number of diseases. What word or phrase can be repeated? For Christians he makes some suggestions that are supported by the Fathers of the Church:

"Lord Jesus, Son of God, have mercy on me a sinner" (Clement, 1995, p. 203)

From Jesus' prayer: "Our Father, who art in heaven" or "Hallowed be Your name" or any short word or phrase from it (Benson, 1984, p. 107)

Any line from the Hail Mary: "Hail Mary, full of grace"

From the Apostles' Creed: "I believe in the Holy Spirit"

"Lord, have mercy."

It is important that they be short so as to be said as you exhale your breath. The ability to mingle the Relaxation Response with your belief system can create powerful internal effects that he terms the "Faith Factor." The two interact mutually to the benefit of one another.

Step Two: Pick up a comfortable posture.

Asian traditions suggest the "lotus" position as one of the many recommended postures for meditation. Being seated cross-legged may not come easy for beginners. Western tradition has developed other forms such as kneeling or standing. Muslims are used to prostration. The idea of sitting at the edge of a chair with the spinal column in the upright position is highly recommended by many mystical traditions because it is believed to make concentration of mind more effective. Positions that are too comfortable will cause a person to fall asleep. In fact, the practice of these techniques can be used to fall asleep or counter insomnia. Painful postures may subject the body to discomfort. When meditation moves to higher levels the very sleepiness will bring about a focused mental awareness, creating a sense of relaxation that is by far more beneficial to the body than sleep.

Step Three: Keep the eyes closed.

Almost all the major mystical traditions recommend closing the eyes as a way to focus and keep from being distracted by usual worries of daily life. It should not be a very uncomfortable squeeze of the eyes but rather very gentle and natural. The atmosphere in the room should not include glaring lights. The dimmer the light, the greater will be the impact.

Step Four: Loosen up your muscles.

Wear loose clothing. Take a few long abdominal breaths, breathing in through the nose and extending the belly. Breathe in through the nose slowly. Hold the air abdominally for some time and breathe out through the mouth. As you hold the air diaphragmatically tighten up your hand and leg muscles and feel the tension. Release the air through the mouth loosening up the muscles and feeling a sensation of relaxation. Repeat ten to twenty times. Keep your arms and legs relaxed. Loosen up your neck muscles, stretch your arms, and rotate your neck if it helps you. You can also tighten up each body parts and loosen them, feeling relaxation progressively from head to toe.

Step Five: Become aware of the sensation of air passing through your nostrils for a while. Gradually, begin repeating your focus word or phrase slowly.

Before introducing your focus word, feel the coolness of the air flowing into the nose and its warmth as it exits. Breathe in freshness and breathe out worries and anxiety. Breathe normally and naturally. You could observe the natural rhythm of your breathing or make your own rhythm. You could be silent when you breathe in and repeat your word or phrase as you exhale. Mystical traditions permit repetition of mantras during both incoming and outgoing breaths. Let your breathing be gentle, natural, and slow. Repetition of a mantra can also be synchronized with your heart beat if it helps you. Visualization of a scene from Holy Scriptures, or an icon or statue can be combined with repetition of the mantra. Details of the visualizations such as color, grace, smell, surroundings, etc., may be observed in detail. Look at the mental picture from top to bottom or from the bottom up gradually. Repetition can be vocal and/or mental. It is better if it starts out vocal and then becomes mental as the mind settles in. Borysenko (2007) recommends simple exercises she calls "The Anytime Series" and/or "The Full-Body Relaxer Series" that anybody can do each day sitting in a chair at home or at the office for twenty minutes (pp. 77-91). These or similar exercises could precede meditation. They will deepen a sense of relaxation and make the meditation more focused.

Step Six: Retain an optimistic, passive, warm, and nonjudgmental attitude.

As you recite your chosen word, phrase, or prayer it is possible that extraneous thoughts will enter your mind. Do not resist thoughts or emotions that occur to you but instead be passive. Observe them gently and perhaps give each a name and then let it go. What is insisted upon is likely to be resisted by the conscious mind. The mind can only be tricked into focus indirectly and not forced into concentration aggressively. Mere repetition will eventually drum the mind and get it centered on the stimulus word. Preceding abdominal breathing exercises provide oxygen or "brain food" to the brain and muscle stretching exercises relax the nervous system, creating a feeling of calm. When mind wandering occurs, gently return to your mantra. It is not about how well you do it but rather that you just do it, no matter if the entire time is spent with distractions. Judging or evaluating performance will only further stimulate the thinking mind instead of calming it.

Step Seven: Let it continue for a specified period of time.

How long should it last? It is better to start out with only ten minutes daily for a period of four weeks. During the period something will resonate deeply. How the mechanism works can be understood more through verifying one's own personal experience. After that it can go anywhere from ten to twenty minutes. Since the meditation is supposed to calm one down it is important that coming out of it not be done under shocking conditions such as an alarm clock. A watch or clock in sight that you see out of the corner of your eye may be helpful. Once the set period of time is over, stop the repetition and remain silent with the eyes closed for a minute or two. Let normal thoughts of consciousness gradually come to you before you open your eyes and gently relax yourself. Many traditions suggest that the mantra be recited during the rest of the day during normal activities such as driving, walking, or performing household chores. The effects of meditation will be transferred to whatever activity is performed and reinforce the calm and focus the meditation caused.

Step Eight: Exercise meditation twice daily.

It is best if the practitioner tries it once daily for four weeks and then twice daily thereafter. The initial four week period is a time to discover its efficacy personally. The specific time of the day to meditate is your choice. But it is highly effective if performed as soon as you get up, before your mind is engrossed with the mundane business of life. Physiological conditions verified by clinical studies advocate an empty stomach or one no more than half full. During meditation, blood flow is directed away from the abdomen to the skin, forearm and leg muscles, and brain. After eating, blood flow centers on the abdominal region, which is counterproductive. Following the natural rhythm of the body will further facilitate the Relaxation Response. Meditating before eating or hours after a meal will produce more benefits. Meditation during fasting will be highly effective for the same reason.

A Much Shorter Version

Time magazine published an interesting special issue on "The Science of Meditation" (Biema, Bjerklie, Cullotta, Park, & McDowell, 2003). The reporters researched the impact of Eastern meditation on the brain and nervous system in their article, "Just Say OM." The article reports that neuroscientists who investigated the impact of meditation on the brain were able to scan and measure changes in the frontal and parietal lobes. It suggests a "teach yourself four-step method" for simple meditation practice to effect measurable physiological change (p. 52).

Step 1: Choose a quiet place.

Switch off lights. It may be less distracting. The less the stimulation from the sensory world, the greater will be the focus.

Step 2: Keep your eyes closed.

Close your eyes. Many religious and mystical traditions advocate shutting the eyes fully or at least partly. It amounts to turning off your brain to process actively the data generated by the senses.

Step 3: Select a word, any word.

Choose a word, phrase, or sound that personally resonates with you, something that may be calming, rhythmic.

Step 4: Begin saying it again and again.

Repeat the chosen word or phrase aloud first and then mentally. It is the boredom of repetition that focuses the mind.

Stein details the results of research by neuroscientists who were able to notice deactivation of the frontal areas of the brain responsible for conscious thought through brain imaging enhanced by injecting a radioactive dye intravenously. He cites studies showing how meditation can boost the immune system and resets the brain to reduce stress. More and more physicians recommend meditation as a way to prevent or slow down the progress of chronic diseases such as cancer, infertility, and AIDS. It also alleviates psychiatric disturbances such as depression, anxiety, hyperactivity, and attention deficit disorder (ADD).

Thomas Keating, a Cistercian monk, has been one of the founding members of a worldwide prayer movement in the Catholic Church called "Centering Prayer." His succinct method involving meditation supports what has been authenticated by people in the medical field. Like the Time magazine's short version, his Christian prayer method that he attributes to an ancient form of prayer method, originally introduced by the author of The Cloud of Unknowing (Walsh, 1981) in the fourteenth century, proposes very similar steps.

Keating introduces the four-step method in his book, Open Mind, Open Heart (1986, pp. 139-141).

Step 1: Select a sacred word as the sign of your objective to surrender to God's presence and action within.

The word has to be chosen prayerfully. Examples: Lord, Jesus, Abba, Father, Mother, Love, Peace, Shalom, Mercy. Keeping up the same word during the entire time is essential to avoid a wandering mind. For some people an inward gaze may be helpful. The gaze, I believe, could be an image of a holy person or icon as a point of focus.

Step 2: Being seated comfortably and with eyes closed, quiet down momentarily. Start silently reciting the sacred word as the sign of your consent to God's presence and action within.

Sitting comfortably means moderate posture. It cannot be so cozy as to fall asleep immediately. Keeping one's back straight contributes to effective concentration. Prayer immediately after a meal will lead to drowsiness. Meditation before sleep may cause insomnia although this can also very well lead one to fall asleep easily. Closing of the eyes enables an inward focus rather than being drawn to what is around us.

Step 3: If you become aware of thoughts, quietly return to focus on your sacred word.

The word "thoughts" may encompass a whole gamut of things such as ideas, emotions, perceptions, memories, images, reflections, and commentaries. Getting caught by these will make the prayer experience ineffective. Forcing them out of the mind is impossible. Not making any effort at all to curb them will lead to dwelling on them. Keep returning gently to the focus word and distractions will eventually fade away. Rather than being aggressive or forceful, one is expected to make the least effort.

Step 4: Once the period of time is over, keep the eyes closed for a few more minutes before becoming aware of the environment.

Twenty minutes, twice daily is the suggested time. An individual may watch a clock out of the corner of an eye. If performed collectively the group leader may say, very slowly, the Our Father or Hail Mary as a gentle reminder to wrap up. The extra minutes are to enable the psyche to reenter the external world of the senses without racing out of the internal world of prayer.

Brain Hemisphere Studies and Meditation

The large cerebral cortex of the brain is divided into two hemispheres, left and right. Although there has been some new research, studies on the lateralization of the brain have broadly distinguished two distinct roles of the left and right hemispheres. The left hemisphere, which controls the right side of the body, is associated with language and logical activities. The right hemisphere, which activates the left side of the body, is responsible for "spatial, simultaneous, and artistic abilities" (Ornstein, 1986, p. 90). The left hemisphere is primarily responsible for analytical, logical thinking, particularly, verbal and arithmetical skills. It operates in a linear way, processing information sequentially.

As the left hemisphere controls speech and logic, the right hemisphere seems specialized for "synthesis." Its communication is limited in the sense that it expresses itself in symbols and mental imagery, bringing before the mind's eye the sensory experiences of touching, seeing, smelling, tasting, and hearing. This hemisphere is "responsible for orientation in space, artistic endeavor, crafts, body image, and recognition of faces" (Ornstein, 1986, p. 91). It processes information more diffusively than the left hemisphere. It is programmed to handle varied inputs simultaneously. If the left hemisphere is logical and sequential, the right hemisphere is "holistic and relational, and more simultaneous in its mode of operation" (Ornstein, 1986, p. 91). It is this part of the brain where consciousness is not logically active but remains very passive and merely receptive.

Meditation shifts an active and externally-oriented consciousness to an internal focus of attention, making it more receptive and quiescent. It turns off attention to the external events of daily life in order to move to an internal quiet where a more comprehensive and complementary knowledge may be passively received. As the dominant, left hemisphere seems to play a major role in consciousness, the right hemisphere plays a subordinate role that is perhaps deeper and subtly powerful. The left hemisphere is associated with the conscious mind and the right hemisphere seems to be related to the unconscious, which is more extensive than the conscious mind. Awareness is not just limited to the conscious mind but moves beyond to a realm that has various deeper levels and is identified by as the unconscious. From Ornstein's study, we can postulate that it is through the activation of the right hemisphere that we can gently override the very active left hemisphere's influence to slip into deeper and more comprehensive levels of consciousness, moving from the conscious mind to the unconscious. "It is a mode of consciousness that is arational, predominantly spatial rather than temporal, and receptive as opposed to active, and it is this 'mode of experience' that is predominantly cultivated in the esoteric traditions" (Ornstein, 1986, p. 182).

Eastern meditators practice methods that seem to contribute to an alteration of consciousness. Their practices demonstrate how through deep meditation they are able to affect and control "involuntary" physiological processes such as blood flow, heart rate, digestive and regenerative activities, breathing, and so on (Ornstein, 1986, p. 194). Generally speaking, medical scientists believe these are unalterable activities that cannot be controlled by the conscious mind. Feats such as being buried alive for days under mud, being submerged in water for several hours, walking barefoot on hot coals, and stopping breathing for a considerable amount of time have been demonstrated by yoga masters defying long-held scientific beliefs.

Study of the Central Nervous System

The central nervous system has two main divisions: sympathetic or voluntary and autonomic or involuntary. The sympathetic nervous system, which is voluntary, controls and coordinates muscles and the movements and postures of the body. The autonomic system, which is involuntary, controls spontaneous functions such as gastrointestinal, vascular, reproductive, and digestive activities that are beyond volitional control. The relationship between mind and body is a well-known and tangible experience. When we experience fear, the body responds to it by feeling butterflies in the stomach. Rapid breathing, fast heart rate, and terrible sweating are symptoms of the body's response to fear perceived by the mind. In the 1920s, W. B. Cannon, a renowned American physiologist who studied the sympathetic nervous system, identified it as the "fight and flight" response (Samuels & Samuels, 1975, p. 219). Adrenaline is pumped into the bloodstream stimulated by the sympathetic part of the autonomous nervous system.

Benson's studies have shown that the relaxation response causes these vital functions of the sympathetic section of the nervous system to be slowed down by practicing autogenic training, yoga, or transcendental meditation. Reduced heart rate, decreased consumption of oxygen, and decreased activity of the autonomic nervous system are called the "integrated response" of the body to the effects of the relaxation factor (Samuels & Samuels, 1975, p. 222). Meditation ultimately can have an important role in treating conditions such as hypertension, caused by excessive stimulation of the sympathetic nervous system.

If the autonomic nervous system is involuntary, then it is perhaps activated by the unconscious mind that is beyond the control of the conscious mind. Right hemisphere functions may be maximized to exert control over the involuntary nervous system. The autonomic nervous system is manipulated by the mind when thinking is quieted by meditation methods. Since all parts of the body are connected directly or indirectly through the central nervous system, there is potential for the entire body to be affected by changes in the autonomic nervous system.

Abdominal breathing contributes large quantities of oxygen as food to the brain which becomes energized. Diaphragmatic breathing also has an impact on the central nervous system, producing a state of relaxation. Studies done on babies reveal the way they relax while they enjoy deep sleep. Prolonged belly breathing causes the diaphragm to extend as far as possible. The nervous system is made to relax by this diaphragm extension. These exercises could be part of or precede meditation in order for the Relaxation Response to impact the body and enhance the Faith Factor.

Contemplative prayer exercises have a tendency to calm the mind because of their repetitiveness. Repetition focuses the mind. Buddhists call this "one-pointedness of mind."

Hindus believe concentration on a single point is essential to contemplation. Focus of mind cannot be achieved by force of will but can only be elicited indirectly. It is amazing to know that such a sophisticated human mechanism as the brain quiets down in response to very silly, monotonous repetition. The mind is "drummed" into focusing on one thing rather than on the many natural distractions of daily life. Just as listening to soft, repetitive music lulls one into a relaxed state, recitation of the same syllable, word, or phrase lulls the mind into a calm but focused state. Babies more easily fall asleep listening to a lullaby. Concentration on one stimulus leads the mind beyond itself to spacelessness, mindlessness, thoughtlessness. It seems very much like the working of the right brain hemisphere that gradually takes control over the left. The deeper part of the mind known as the unconscious is perhaps activated through these exercises to which the right hemisphere responds more readily than the left which is actively engaged with constant thoughts and active processes (Amalraj, 2002). Who knows what the extent of our being is? Are there areas far deeper than just the conscious mind and even the unconscious, the extended part of the mind, over which neither the conscious mind nor the unconscious has absolute control? The possibilities are unlimited.

Psychological Studies on Levels of Being

The past century has witnessed investigations into the human psyche much more deeply and broadly than in previous centuries. Psychological studies exploded with the advent of psychoanalysis, a theory that analyzes the human psyche from Freud's perspectives. Sigmund Freud is generally known as the father of modern psychology. His contribution of the notion of the unconscious remains substantial to inquiry into the human mind. Psychology is the study of the human mind. Modern medical science studying physiology is greatly assisted by psychological studies. Today mind/body connections are clinically examined both by physicians and psychologists.

In the preceding section we saw how the left and right hemispheres function differently. Each is in charge of two opposite patterns of functioning. While the left is responsible for dominant activities such as logical thinking, language, calculation and analysis, the right is involved in artistic, imaginative, special, and simultaneous activities. While the conscious mind is believed to be associated with left hemisphere activities, the unconscious mind may be related to the right hemisphere which performs nondominant, yet very significant functions. The nondominant right hemisphere is usually known as "minor" but in fact subtly and gently calms down, quiets, and controls the left brain. But the extent of human existence goes far beyond both the conscious and unconscious mind (Ornstein, 1986).

Freud's psychoanalysis examined the human psyche and postulated the existence of the unconscious mind. According to Freud, behavior is "determined by psychic energies such as irrational forces, unconscious motivations and conflicts, biological and instinctual drives, and certain psychosexual events during the first six years of life" (Corey, 1977, p. 96). For Freud "consciousness is the thin slice of the total mind" (p. 98). The larger part of the mind exists below the surface of awareness like the greater part of an iceberg lies underwater. It cannot be accessed directly but only indirectly through dreams, slips of the tongue, and other ways such as free association. The unconscious stores "all experiences, memories, and repressed materials" (p. 98). Needs and motivations that are outside the realm of awareness are beyond conscious control. "Most psychological functioning exists in the out-of-awareness realm" (p. 98). The goal of psychoanalytic theory is to make unconscious motives conscious so that one can exercise choice, free from interference. Even though the unconscious is beyond awareness it does influence behavior significantly. Unconscious forces are the root causes of all forms of neurotic symptoms and behaviors. "Repressed materials that interfere with healthy functioning" need to be uncovered and released in order for a person to experience healing (Corey, 1977, p. 98).

Freud's investigations inaugurated an era of psychological inquiry. Many other theories followed either expanding on or contradicting his claims. Since his time, there have been three other major theories, or "forces," in the field of psychology: behavioral, humanistic, and transpersonal. Behavioral studies disclaimed the unconscious and focused on external behavior to help alleviate personality problems. Humanistic investigations disagreed with treating human beings as objects of study by behaviorists. Instead, humanists studied ways of being present to patients with genuine, unconditional, positive regard so as to offer a climate in which change would be effected from within. But by the end of the past century and the turn of this century, "Transpersonal Psychology" or "Psychospirituality" has emerged as one of the four major forces of psychology.

Transpersonal psychology encompasses the whole person and beyond. Humans are parts of a whole. Since consciousness itself is inside as well as outside of awareness, it should include not only what is within a person but what is outside. Transpersonal psychology postulates an area that is spiritual in addition to the instinctual identified by Freud. Victor Frankl divides the unconscious into "unconscious instinctuality and unconscious spirituality" (1975, p. 25). It is as if Freud observed only a "negative depository" in the unconscious because his study was concerned primarily with an examination of neurotics. Suppressed and repressed materials are coded into the instinctual part of the unconscious, and they need to be decoded by bringing them forth gently and indirectly to awareness. Otherwise, they affect current behaviors adversely. But human beings experience positive feelings such as love, peace, joy, forgiveness, and compassion simultaneously with negative emotions such as anger, anxiety, depression, helplessness, and so on. Just as there is a negative depository, the positive or healthy experiences such as love, peace, and joy must also be coded in the "positive depository" of the unconscious (Amalraj, 2002). A journey to the positive spiritual part of the unconscious is facilitated by meditative practices.

Freud and Jung as psychoanalysts employed techniques such as free association, dream analysis, and active imagination to get at the instinctual unconscious indirectly because it is beyond the purview of consciousness. Great mystics used prayer exercises to awaken the contemplative mind not to analyze but simply to slip into the healthy spiritual unconscious to experience the indwelling presence of the Absolute. Transpersonal-spiritual approaches state that "through the unconscious a person is connected with the spiritual world. This world can include God, gods, angels, ancestors, and other transpersonal entities, beings, or powers" (Caputi, 1984, pp. 136-7). This approach purports that the unconscious is composed of a substantive transpersonal entity or medium that is able to contact other transpersonal entities. The idea is similar to immanence and transcendence of absolute reality. There is room for connecting to the absolute deep within the unconscious. Christians call it the soul. Others may term it the spirit.

I do believe that human beings can move from the conscious mind to the instinctual unconscious to the spiritual unconscious. There are layers in the unconscious. The unconscious contains within itself a "higher state of awareness or spiritual consciousness" (Assagioli, 1965, p. 129). This area is what I call "the state of unconditional love." It is an area that is unknown and yet it is within the realm of love. It is unknowing love as pointed out in the classic The Cloud of Unknowing (Walsh, 1981). Since it is a state of total acceptance that is beyond knowing, individuals can only surrender to the greatest presence that is already within. The methods employed are not then viewed as an entitlement but merely an attempt to be calm, surrender, and be receptive to what is freely, gratuitously given. Because this experience cannot be attained through human intelligence, one must follow nonrational methods such as repetition of a word or phrase with faith. The right hemisphere of the brain appears to calm down left hemisphere's dominant, articulate functions only to activate a passive, receptive, and quiescent mode of being. The meditative methods seem to quiet even the involuntary nervous system, to be open to influence far more calming than its own functions can achieve.

Concentration Versus Relaxation

Contemplative prayer methods and exercise seem to lead to a focusing of the mind during which one also experiences a great sense of relaxation. In this state of relaxation it seems that individuals move beyond the personal unconscious to more comprehensive mode of the unconscious. Jung would term this the "collective unconscious." It is a spiritual reality, common to all and yet unknown to us, but has existed in humans since the beginning of the species (Sandford, 1997). There are two identified layers of this deeper unconscious mode: instinctual and spiritual. The spiritual realm of the unconscious is not only individual but also collective, transcending the personal. It is unique to each person and yet simultaneously linked to all. Although many, we are one, says St. Paul. There is one God but Three Persons. Since a deliberate, conscious attempt cannot transport one to the personal and collective spiritual realm of the unconscious, a simple repetition of words and phrases is employed to drum the more active part of the left hemisphere of the brain into silence. The process appears to be activated by the right hemisphere using simple, monotonous methods of constant recitation. The exercise appears to activate the right hemisphere just as the dominant left hemisphere activity shuts down. A person then moves from conscious mind to the unconscious where both unhealthy and healthy materials are stored. There is a movement from unhealthy instinctual materials to the healthy spiritual unconscious, commonly identified as a state of "unconditional love." It is in this state that the human soul merges with the Absolute.

The key seems to be concentration which leads to a deep focused state of mind. Does the meditative exercise produce a focused state of mind? Or, conversely, does the focused state of mind contribute to effective meditation? I believe they are mutual. It is true one has to focus on the repetition, but the very repetition itself can bring about a focused state of mind. Intense concentration cannot be easily attained by all. Nor should it be forced but rather gently evoked indirectly. It is not so much about how accurately, perfectly, or correctly but rather how persistently one is involved. It is habitual meditation that produces a better outcome in the long run than one perfect meditation. Aiming to be perfect will only awaken the active left part of the brain. Since the intention is to gradually subdue the cognitive mind and let the perceptive mind arise, the exercise needs to be gentle, voluntary, and yet resolute and continual. It is desire that brings a better result than perfection. Someone once said "the desire to pray is to pray."

The many methods suggested using various mystical and religious traditions seem to fall into two different categories: one that uses sensations that arise from five senses: sight, touch, taste, smell, and hearing; and another that employs mental imagery, that is, when these five sensations are brought before the mind's eye. Repeating or chanting of a mantra for example, a word such as "Jesus," or a phrase such as "Jesus, Son of God, have mercy on me a sinner," may be said out loud or silently in the mind. When it is recited out loud it is said to be in the auditory sensory mode, and the silent mental invocation is its counterpart in the imagery mode. Observing a holy picture in detail may be using the visual sensory mode and its mental viewing is visualization or the mental imagery mode. One may hear a waterfall in nature or listen imaginatively to the sound of the waves. One may walk on the ground feeling one's feet touch the ground, sit on a sofa or chair and feel one's back and thighs touching the furniture, or one can touch water, sand, or other objects mentally. A person can walk into a garden and look at every flower and smell their fragrance and be completely attuned to the process. The same experience can be experienced mentally. More than one sensation and/or mental image may be combined to reinforce concentration. The meditative process is involved in either one or simultaneously in both of the modes. Repetition in the auditory and mental imagery mode is most common and easy but certainly it can be enhanced if other modes, such as visual, auditory, or mental are combined. For example, as the person repeats the mantra with the eyes closed, visualization of a deity such as the Sacred Heart of Jesus may be visualized in detail at the same time. It will enhance the focus of the mind.

What happens when sensations and/or the mental imagery mode are exercised? What effect does repetition of any word or action in these two modes produce? A deliberate focus on an internal or external stimulus creates what is called one-pointedness of mind during which a person moves from the conscious mind to the unconscious to the spiritual unconscious. Normal consciousness is unfocused, erratic, and automatic. Breathing is shallow and irregular or unrhythmic. The conscious state can create anxiety by allowing the mind to be focused on needless worries. Psychophysical exercises such as abdominal breathing and muscle tension and relaxation exercises can produce a focused mind. Further, meditative practices lead to fresh perceptions. Obsession with thoughts is broken. Unimpeded by prior perceptions, ever new, unclouded, unbiased perceptions start to emerge. It makes room for religious or mystical experiences. The word enlightenment or illumination often refers to the progress made in these disciplines. In psychological terms the progression is known as "deautomatization, an undoing of the normal automatization of consciousness" (Ornstein, 1986, p. 197). The ultimate level of this experience culminates in a heightened awareness of a presence or moment. It is so deep and so fulfilling that it is a sort of "nothingness experience." Subject-object separation disappears. It is comparable to the stage of Samadhi of the Indian Royal Yoga. In that deep meditative state, the mind still thinks but of no thing. The soul is gifted with the "paradox of seeing the invisible" (Smith, 1991, p. 49). It is empty and at the same time the void is filling, being deeply satiated. This greatest love can be responded to by simply being present to it unpretentiously without thoughts or feelings to translate it. One can merely surrender, empty oneself, to the all-filling, satiating experience of God's unconditional love.

Simply persisting in these methods carries one beyond effort-taking. It usually starts with much effort only to transcend the very effort in order to become completely effortless whereby one realizes it is simply a given and not an acquired state. The method which starts out as a means eventually becomes an end in itself. The very prayer that is effort-filled becomes a liberating, effortless experience of love. To pray then is to love and to love is to pray. This is the secret of contemplative meditation methods. For human beings, a reward very often follows an action. But in this form of prayer the very action itself becomes its own reward. The present and the future melt into timelessness. The states of acting and being in the world then become one and the same. These exercises can transport one to a state of being apart from doing. Being and acting merge into one. After that, abundant actions might follow this very extraordinary experience of being in communion with the Absolute and the world. Actions for God and others will be multiplied as opposed to being measured out in response to laws. The separation between the now and the later simply disappears. It is an experience of timelessness, spacelessness. The future is experienced in the now. It ends in the union of the self with the Self. It is the union of the soul with God. The kingdom of God is present now in one's heart.

Contemplative meditation methods lead to mystical, religious experiences that reassure one of God's indwelling presence deep in the soul. William James (1890, quoted and interpreted in Ornstein, 1986, p. 198) characterized the above-mentioned deeply transformative experiences as having four distinguishing features unique to religious experience. 1) Unity or oneness: Experience becomes more comprehensive than fragmented; associations between things by and large disconnected are seen as related. Experiencing self as one with the cosmos and God is uniquely perceived. Separation between self and the world is gently merged into a union with God. "Many" is perceived as one, just as the Three Persons of the Holy Trinity are one God. It defies the logically thinking and analytically computing mind. 2) A sense of realness becomes intense. No matter how the impact of prayer practices may be described to non-practitioners it will still be unreal and beyond their experience. A person has to experience it in order to understand and make it real.

This is not evidence of the efficacy of prayer practices, but rather a deep conviction that the experience is personal and verifiable from within. It no longer needs to be forced. However, there is nothing in outer reality to confirm this inner experience. 3) Ineffability: The outcome of the prayer experience is so deep that it is impossible to describe, articulate, or explain. A real experience differs totally from that of any sense perception or an idea. Therefore, it is hard to put it into words. "Incommunicableness" is the condition of this state of being. The person feels a loss of words to reveal what is experienced. The result is absolute silence. 4) Passivity: Although the process involves the practitioner's voluntary exercises, such as the repetition of a word or phrase to focus on a single point or source, the outcome in the final analysis seems so involuntary, unearned, unmerited, and undeserved. Once the spiritual unconscious comes to consciousness the person's will seems to be in abeyance, as though grasped by a superior power (James, 1982, p. 381). To borrow St. Paul's words, "no longer I, but Christ lives in me" (Gal 2:20).

Falling into the deepest part of our being is a journey to the soul where there is the indwelling presence of God. Communion with God cannot be earned through morality although morality is a prerequisite. It is a journey of deep faith in which you simply trust the presence of God and be present to it. It is a realization of not what you do but what is being done to you by God. That is why when Mary realized everything from God was pure unearned mercy, she said, "Let it be done to me according to your word." Since God's love is unconditional you can only simply receive it. What you need to do is not do anything at all. Learning not to do anything or to let go is difficult because we would rather do something that is harder than not to do anything, which is the easiest of all. Letting the dominant mind rest and waking up the heart is not easy. It is too simple and uncomplicated but human intelligence is more used to performing complex actions in order to achieve and accomplish.

The techniques exercised by mystics are mere monotony and boredom, which the intelligent human mind will resist and may even become fearful and anxious. But to one who has learned the art of surrendering, every repetitious word or phrase sounds as if it were new. The greatest love of God may be missed by many not because it is difficult or requires sophisticated understanding but precisely because it is least demanding, least complicated, least conditioning, and least coercive. But then you are gifted with the extraordinary freedom to perform more than what is required or expected of you. Contemplative meditation enables one to think not with the head but with the heart. Persevering in these methods makes one connect to deeper layers of meanings usually unperceived by actively thinking consciousness. Deeper and deeper meanings of sacred words and events are not intellectually perceived through discursive processes but rather the devotee waits patiently for meaning to be revealed from deep within the soul. Continued practice of these exercises will enable one to grasp what is called the symbolic or spiritual meanings of the Scriptures that are far deeper than literal, moral, or historical meanings. Inspiration has not so much to do with new knowledge as it does with old information suddenly becoming new. The old suddenly glows with new meaning. In the following section different layers of meanings in sacred scripture will be analyzed.

Chapter III

Mystical Meaning and Mystics

In our interactions with one another we use words to convey our ideas, perceptions, understandings, and feelings. Many times we mean what we say. But sometimes we use figures of speech to convey something different from what the words themselves say. The "straw that broke the camel's back" is just such a use of language that has both literal and symbolic meanings. If a camel's back is overloaded by just one more bit of weight such as a straw, it might collapse. But figuratively, the expression refers to a small but significant piece of information that tips the balance for me. I reach a boiling point where I start reacting because I cannot take it anymore. The expression "dragging my feet" does not literally allude to the dragging of my feet in dealing with a particular issue or responsibility. If indeed I had such a problem, it would certainly mean what it says in its literal sense. But rather I use the expression to convey how I am reluctant to pursue a particular path of action or to deal with some designated responsibility.

As believers we constantly encounter symbolism in matters of faith. Sacraments are full of symbolism and yet we believe they are also real, conferring upon us graces when we participate. The Eucharist is not simply bread and wine; it is the body and blood of Jesus Christ. It is a meal as well as a sacrifice Jesus offered on Calvary. It symbolizes an eternal banquet in heaven where God will satiate our desires and cravings. It is also a celebration of communion with God, one another, angels, and those who have departed this world before us. The water we use in baptism symbolizes the washing away of our sins and anointing, the outpouring of the Holy Spirit. John's gospel and the synoptics are full of symbolism. Scholars and saints believe that there are deeper, interior, psychological, and esoteric meanings in the gospel narratives (Sanford, 1997). Jesus himself uses symbolic language: I am the bread of life, resurrection and life, Good Shepherd, Living Water, Light of the World, the Way, the Truth, and Life, the vine and the branches, etc.

Allegorically, he portrays God as a sower, landowner, father of the prodigal son, wine grower, and so on.

Literal, Moral, Allegorical, and Unitive Meanings

The Fathers of the early Church, in particular Origen, believed the scriptures contained both literal and spiritual meanings. While the literal can be understood in the historical composition of the narratives, the spiritual sense cannot be understood unless its symbolism is examined. While modern interpreters explain the word of God from purely materialistic and rationalistic points of view, ancient commentators "gazed inward into the world of the soul" to look for "profound and meaningful but irrational ways" (Sanford, 1997, p. 2). As we have been informed by medical science and psychology, the right hemisphere is the area of the brain that contains the nonrational part of our consciousness, complementing the left hemisphere's active thinking. It is a part of a deeper and more comprehensive knowledge that is beyond expression and yet significantly complementary to inner harmony.

The early Christian interpreters of the Bible, such as Gregory of Nyssa, were opposed to interpreting the Bible from a merely literal or historical perspective, disregarding its spiritual meaning. In fact, they believed that the Bible could not be fully comprehended if the spiritual meanings were not taken into consideration. The language of scripture is seen by mystical tradition as something that reveals without revealing; something that conceals and at the same time offers hints (Stroumsa, 1996). Jesus himself does not teach everything to everybody. He offers limited words in the parable of the sower but explains it in detail to his disciples privately. He himself alludes to the hidden meanings of his words: "Knowledge of the mysteries of the kingdom of God has been granted to you; but to the rest, they are made known through parables so that 'they may look but not see, and hear but not understand'" (Lk 8: 9-10). Many of us deal with sacred scripture in the same way today because even though we hear it over and over again, we do not understand its deeper meanings.

Keating (1994) discusses the four meanings of sacred scripture: literal, moral, allegorical, and unitive. These are not four ways in the sense of being totally different from one another but rather in the sense of different layers of listening. First, literal: It is the historical message that is of interest. Facts and figures are examined literally. Under what circumstances did Jesus say what he did and what did it mean to the people of that era? What were the geographical locations where the individuals moved from place to place? What meanings do the passages convey literally? This undertaking arises from a philosophical and analytic purpose for the sake of gathering information.

Second, moral: Once the literal meaning is understood, the next task is to apply it to our lives and follow it. Ethical standards such as canon law are drawn from the words and deeds of Jesus. We do not just listen to Jesus but also put his teaching into action. When we read and reflect upon the words of Jesus, we try to connect them to our own standards and keep them as norms. The sacred word becomes the measuring rod by which we evaluate our lives, correct our behaviors, and abide by God's will. It sets ethical standards of directing and guiding. God's word becomes the way when I am wayward, light when I live in darkness, and hope when I am in despair. It enables me now to trust God's will as revealed by his Son.

Third, allegorical: This stage appears to be a natural progression from the previous two. In the previous two levels, understanding of the sacred word may be superficial, external, and impersonal. I try to control my life from without. I follow the rules and regulations of morality. Everything is made to look correct, exact, perfect, and wonderful externally without necessarily being personal. As Paul experienced even in following the law faithfully, one can end up hurting someone. He persecuted Christians even though he had strictly followed the norms of Orthodox Judaism. He only exercised an external locus of control that ultimately failed him. In doing everything right, he found in fact that he was wrong. When the sacred word was written it was not meant to report simply what occurred or what was spoken to the people of that era. The words of Jesus were related several decades after his mortal existence and were appropriate to people's ongoing struggles then and even to the present day. They were recalled and composed as the message reflected the conditions of the lives of different Christian communities. Jesus' message transcends time and applies to all who lived then, who live now, and who will be living in the future. It is something that resonates within us and with which we can have a personal connection. At this stage we interiorize the sacred word and draw personal meanings from it. Events, such as the crossing of the Red Sea by the Israelites, are observed more like personal experiences. The liberation from Egyptian slavery may resonate with my being released from addictive behaviors by God. Historical happenings assume a personal perspective.

The fourth, unitive: The inward movement becomes more pronounced at this level when reading and reflecting upon the word of God. When you are immersed in the word of God, it captures your attention in a very profound way. On the unitive level, you relate to the events even more personally than at the allegorical level. You become the actor, composer, and writer, staging the word of God scripted for your personal life story. The sacred word and you become one and the same. John Cassian says while sometimes you chant or recite a psalm, you sometimes feel as though you composed it yourself. You feel as though you have become the mouthpiece of God, speaking for God. This translates into extraordinary union with God. But this does not happen before some unloading of the unconscious happens at the allegorical level. Darker unresolved materials get flushed out as we continue to sustain contemplation of God's word. It occurs naturally and indirectly. Materials that interfere with our behaviors are unleashed from the negative depository of the unconscious. In the fourth level, one moves to the deepest or highest level of consciousness, that is, the spiritual unconscious. Here one experiences the Promised Land after crossing over and leaving behind the slavery of sin. This is where peace and joy overflow in one's heart due to communion with God.

What we see on different levels of the journey is a gradual progression from a conscious, intellectual process, to the deep inner part of our problems-storing negative instinctual unconscious, to the positive depository of the spiritual unconscious where love, peace, and joy are indwelling because of the unearned presence of the Absolute. But the way the monks of earlier centuries experienced this journey was not necessarily by reflecting the scriptures discursively. In fact, analyzing how monks stumbled upon this union, Keating relates how they had to memorize the scripture for lack of enough manuscript. Their participation in the liturgy of the hour called for recitation of psalms and scripture passages. To store them in memory, they recited passages privately to themselves while they indulged in manual labor. Surprisingly enough, they experienced an inward movement whereby the sacred word began to speak to them through an unknowing inner journey that was far more powerful than intellectual processes. A simple repetition made a tremendous difference in their lives. What we see here is that a simple repetition of God's word in deep faith brought about a deep transformation. It is as if they moved with God's word from the head to the heart. They discovered a way of listening not just with the head but also with the heart. Listening with their hearts brought about a stronger transformation than reflective exercises did.

In order for one to understand the deeper layers of the word of God it is necessary to practice contemplative meditation. Once a quieting down of the mind takes place, rather than actively understanding its meaning from a rational perspective, the heart simply receives what is being freely offered. At this stage, one wakes up the receptive mode of the right brain which receives information that cannot be processed by the left cerebral hemisphere. It is beyond the purview of the thinking and analyzing left brain. Once a person learns to sustain these methods, layers and layers of the word of God previously unrevealed and unknown will be unveiled. One will be able to understand or interpret the scripture paradoxically. Paradox is juxtaposing opposites. It is holding together opposites. Now a person can become comfortable with a statement that is both true and false at the same time. Contradicting statements do not confuse. Understanding and unknowing coexist. Mystery and reality are held together preciously. One divine Being at the same time being three no longer confounds. "How can a man, who suffered terribly, at the same time be the Son of God?" is no longer something that I need to understand because I only need to believe out of love. I do not need to understand to love, but I can love to understand.

Contemplative Meditation Leading to the Unitive Level

In a nutshell, we see repetition of a word or phrase recited out loud or silently leading to a deep, inner experience making the mind become very focused in concentration. Effort-filled concentration leads to an effortless focus of mind. I would now like to highlight how to practice more than what to practice. Repetition of sound happens in one or two ways: auditory sensory and/or mental imagery form. Only one sensation out of five, hearing, is commonly applied. Although the impact of the method has been verified by medical science and transpersonal psychology, mystical traditions from the major world religions offer a variety of choices employing more of the five sensations in the sensory and mental imagery form. Why? The key is to make the mind focused through concentration on a single point or source. After that, even the method becomes irrelevant once contemplation reaches its deepest level. With one's personal faith as a guiding force, the very practice of faith then becomes an extraordinary experience of love. In the following section I would like to highlight how Christian mystical traditions, from the early Fathers of the Church to the fifteenth-century mystics, used a combination of the senses and imagination of sensations in contemplative meditation.

Mystical traditions start with the words and deeds of Jesus. Jesus himself says his words contain deeper meanings. In the simple keeping of his words in the heart, one will understand their deeper meanings. Jesus says, "Whoever loves me will keep my word, and my Father will love him, and we will come to him and make our dwelling with him" (Jn 14: 23). God is the revealer of all secrets. According to St. Augustine, divine secrets are "hidden in the depth of the soul," and by resting in God they are unveiled. The gospels tell us that Jesus himself spent many nights praying to his Father all alone on the mountain to discern God's will. He prayed all night alone before making significant choices such as selecting his apostles. We see long praying being linked to serious decisions Jesus made. His close relationship with the Father reveals many secrets to humanity. The Kingdom of God, Jesus says, lies deep within human hearts, and we can enter into it here on earth. Our idea of heaven is that it is not of this world and not in our lifetime. Heavenly life and eternity and even resurrection are already available for us to choose, believe, and act upon. Jesus says, "Whoever eats my flesh and drinks my blood has eternal life, and I will raise him on the last day" (Jn 6: 54). Thus Jesus assures his believers of heaven here on earth now as well as in the future. The inner eyes called "eyes of faith" that enable one to live that future reality now can be opened here on earth in a prayerful relationship with God.

Concentration techniques developed with Patristic Tradition and the Fathers of the Egyptian desert. Focusing attention on prayer deepened the impact of meditation and a personal experience of God. The more scattered the attention the less effective it is. Prayer created mental focus. Effective concentration then made prayer desirous. Concentration is required for prayer, and prayer is necessary for mental focus. They are mutually influential, one strengthening the efficacy of the other. Traditionally, a word or phrase from a psalm or personal prayer was repeated. It was not meant as a technique but as an expression of personal love for God. Incidentally, simple recitation controlled the constant flow of thoughts. Steady repetition of a phrase such as "O God, make haste to help me" (NRSV, Ps 70:1) at all times: on journeys, before and during sleep, in the house, walking outside, lying down or rising, centers meditation on God. The words of the blind man, "Lord Jesus, Son of God, have mercy on me a sinner" was also another favorite phrase. Calling upon God was combined rhythmically with breathing. Recitation of Jesus' prayer "Our Father" "without the sound of any voice, without any movement of the tongue, without any articulate word," brought about an "ineffable state that is far above all human feeling" (Cassian, quoted in Clement, 1995, p. 207).

In spiritual exercises simple sensations such as "breathing," "gazing at the majesty of a tree," "touching a stone" or "bark of a tree," smelling the fragrance of a tree, or relishing fruits of a tree meant transcendence for mystics (Clement, 1995, p. 223). The five senses of the body are so consciously employed that they lead to a focusing of the mind. Looking at the human body may engender lust or rather a glimpse into the divine, depending on the perceiver. The sight of a beautiful woman's body brought tears and thoughts of their own beautiful resurrected bodies in heaven (John Climacus in Clement, 1995). The sensation of looking at objects such as the sacred vessels moved monks to experience the presence of God. Their passionate hearts encouraged them to look at birds and animals and sense the presence of the Creator.

St. Francis of Assisi

A beautiful sunset, sun or moon, or anything of beauty in nature transported St. Francis of Assisi into transcendence. Driven by an overwhelming sense of love for the Creator embodied in his creation, he composed the beautiful hymn The Canticle of the Sun, paying tribute to Brother Sun, Sister Moon, Brother Wind, Sister Water, Mother Earth, and even Sister Bodily Death (Harkness, 1973, p. 97). St. Francis would kneel or lie with his arms spread apart, eyes fixed toward heaven, and pray loudly. He bore the suffering of the crucified Jesus in his heart always and wept for Him. He yearned, even begged, for the grace to feel the suffering of Jesus in his own body and soul. With extended and upraised arms like a cross he begged for the gift of the five wounds of Jesus in his body. Body postures and earnest desire in addition to loud, repetitive prayer and the image of the crucifix before his eyes (as well as active imagination) are the keys to St. Francis' profound mystical experience.

St. Catherine of Siena

St. Catherine of Siena exercised an imagery form of prayer inspired by Jesus' words: "The kingdom of God is [within] you" (Lk 17:21). As a young girl Catherine used to have a small and simple room in her beautiful home which she considered her hermitage wherein she would retreat to pray. When her parents intended to give her away in marriage, they prevented her every chance to pray in an attempt to change her mind. Catherine used this opportunity to deepen her union with God by mentally building a hermitage in the recesses of her heart. She called it her cell which is a simple residence hermits used to live in, abandoning all forms of possessions to be wholehearted in their search for a mystical union with God. The monks used to live in the crevices of rocks and deserts and other empty places to seek God. Much of their time was spent in contemplation of God. In her imagination, Catherine would build an immaterial cell and invite her friends to do the same for a deep prayer experience.

As time went on Catherine's imagination expanded. Instead of using a modest inner cell to hide, she began to imagine elaborate dimensions within, and it became the lavish home of God. Her inner dwelling was comprised of two different and yet inseparable chambers: one represented her awareness of herself and the other her knowledge of God. In her communication with the Lord it was revealed that the more she knew of herself in relation to the Lord, the less proud and presumptuous she would be. Self-knowledge by itself would lead only to an inflated ego.

Catherine believed vocal prayer was the beginning of all prayer. Reciting prayers was only a means to focus on the love of God. The mere mouthing of words would accomplish nothing if it did not lead to inner silence. She believed that external prayers were only preparation for the prayer of the heart, which she called "mental prayer." Words and thoughts were merely the first step to the restful silence in which one would not speak or think but just be present to the gift of God's intimate presence. She called this a wordless union, a silent resting in God's presence. It might lead one to experience the sweetness of the Lord or perhaps an apparent dryness and emptiness which she believed were evidence of the Lord's nearness to us. To foster this inner quiet, she often repeated a phrase from Scripture or something that welled up in her heart spontaneously. She continually invoked and repeated phrases such as "Lord have mercy on me," "O God, come to our assistance! Lord, makes haste to help us" and "Gentle Jesus, Jesus love" (Fatula, 1987, p. 98). She moved from vocal prayer to mental prayer within minutes, sometimes even before finishing the Our Father. Repetition of words of faith that started in the sensory mode and moved quickly to mental imagery mode created in her a centering experience. From the active left brain she shifted to the nonactive contemplative mind.

St. Ignatius of Loyola

St. Ignatius of Loyola is acclaimed as one of the great mystics. His life contains a great conversion. He went from being a military soldier to becoming a soldier for Christ. Although born to nobility and dedicated to chivalry, he abandoned his treasured status and committed himself to the Lord. When he read the Life of Christ and the lives of the saints while recovering from wounds suffered in battle, he was given the grace to distinguish between the joy of human pleasures and achievements and the lasting love experienced by contemplating divine matters. He underwent a deep transformation in the cave of Manresa. Recalling his experiences, he was able to compile a set of techniques he called "Spiritual Exercises" for those desirous of experiencing such deep transformation.

It is a guide for a four-week meditation. The first week is dedicated to purifying the soul through sorrow and contrition. The second week centers on the knowledge and love of Jesus by contemplating scenes from his public life. The third comprises reflections on the Passion of Christ. The final week focuses on the resurrection of Jesus leading the retreatants to unselfish love and joy in Christ's glory. In his Exercises we find the use of the five senses and mental imagery that contribute to a centering state.

Ignatius invites the meditators to see with the mind's eye the physical environment in which the meditation occurs. Be it a temple, mountain, or valley, surrounding gospel scenes are detailed and vivid pictorial visualizations. Imagine Christ hanging on the cross and having a conversation concerning the fact that even though he is the Creator he humbled himself to become a man and submit to death on a cross for our sins. What would I do for him? Another meditation may center on the Nativity, recalling how Mary and Joseph traveled on a donkey to Nazareth. Imagine the landscape of mountains and valleys and visualize their travel on a donkey and meditate. Bodily postures such as the closing of eyes, kneeling, prostration on the floor, lying with face upward, standing, seated, and even walking back and forth could be added to facilitate contemplation. These postures in conjunction with the use of the senses make mental imagery much more centering. Deprivations such as closing the shutters, turning off the lights, and closing the door while in contemplation are recommended. Fasting and chastisement of the body such as inflicting pain and wearing hair shirts, cords, or chains further use the sensations to add to mental focusing.

At the end of each section, St. Ignatius recommends the repetition of customary prayers such as the Hail Mary, Our Father, Creed, Soul of Christ, and Hail Holy Queen either vocally or mentally. "With each breath taken in or expelled, one should pray mentally, by saying a word of the Our Father, or of any other prayer which is recited. This is done in such a manner that one word of the prayer is said between one breath and another" (Ganss, 1991, p. 181). Rhythmic breathing also adds to the effectiveness of meditation. A combination of various components of sensory and mental imagery tends to produce an inner silence whereby one becomes passively receptive to the greatest love that is self-existing and spontaneous.

St. Teresa of Avila

St. Teresa of Avila is considered one of the most psychological mystics. Her journey of the imagination reveals deep insights into a mystical union with God. Although she recommended vocal prayer and discursive meditation as a beginning, she was deeply contemplative in her use of mental imagery. Using her imagination she built a crystal palace deep within what she called the Interior Castle, an acclaimed masterpiece in the mystical tradition. It is the journey of a soul in mystical union with God. It consists of seven mansions, each elaborately furnished and surrounded by beautiful gardens with flowers and trees created by "His Majesty," her God. She sees her soul journeying through six types of "dwelling places" before it reaches the Sanctum Sanctorum in the center. After betrothal in the sixth place a spiritual marriage occurs in the seventh, uniting her soul with God. In each stage, the soul grows spiritually before union with the Absolute. Teresa frequently imagines these mansions to facilitate her contemplation. In the journey that she details, one can see the progress of a soul in its stages of growth. The soul can be compared to a traveler who roams among these places before arriving at the center (Kavanaugh & Rodríguez, 1979).

Teresa starts with the environs of a castle that is surrounded by darkness, cold, poisonous snakes, and all sorts of wild beasts. The castle is in the shape of a crystal globe. The rooms of the castle are like the leaves of a palm, arranged in concentric circles around the spacious and lavish center where the King lives. The castle has fountains, gardens, and labyrinths. The first three dwelling places are compared to the stages of active prayer or meditation. The first dwelling place is simply the entrance to the castle. The rest of the places have elaborate upper and lower chambers and gardens. Upon entering the castle one is still exposed to the darkness and cold outside. The fountain and the plants are foul and smelly. People at this stage are still absorbed with worldly possessions, honor, and the daily business of life. Creatures crawl into the rooms from outside the castle. In the second dwelling place, relationship with God becomes somewhat serious because here one responds to spiritual exercises such as reading spiritual books, listening steadily to sermons, enduring illnesses and trials, and moments of prayer actively. An individual's focus on worldly matters is destabilized or de-centered by God's call.

Settling down into a more committed Christian life marks the third place. Prayer becomes an essential part of the soul and dedication to one's faith becomes a role model to fellow Christians. People learn to spend time well and perform works of charity. Some stability enters a person's life. A tendency to remain in this place is a danger to further spiritual development. The fears and anxieties of life interfere and intimidate a person to feel a loss of control of life. At this stage one will be invited by the King to move toward the center through deeper contemplation.

The fourth dwelling place marks a time of transition in the progress of the traveler advancing toward the center. Prayer at this stage becomes less and less discursive or an activity orchestrated by human effort. God draws the soul more and more into an interior state of recollection. The soul becomes receptive to prayer, which is the beginning of contemplation. Recollection characterizing this state is called the "prayer of quiet" in the fourth place (Welch, 1982, p. 19). To differentiate between the meditation exercised in the first three dwelling places and the "contemplative prayer of quiet" in the fourth place, Teresa uses the imagery of two water troughs. In the former, the water comes from a faraway source through long aqueducts with much human effort. This is likened to active prayer. In the latter, the trough is placed on a spring that brings forth water effortlessly. The second trough is compared to contemplative prayer. While active prayer brings forth what Teresa calls consolations, contemplative prayer produces spiritual delights which can only be passively received. "Spiritual delight is not something that can be imagined, because however diligent our efforts we cannot acquire it" (p. 75). The key here is not to think, although recollection of God through thinking is a necessary preliminary. As Teresa says, "One should let the intellect go and surrender oneself in the arms of love" (Kavanaugh & Rodriguez, 1979, p. 81). Teresa refers to the awakening of the contemplative mind associated with the right hemisphere.

The fifth dwelling place represents a deepening contemplative prayer that is termed by Teresa as "prayer of union." In this prayer one encounters an experience of God in which "one neither sees, nor hears, nor understands, because the union is always short and seems to the soul even much shorter than it probably is" (Teresa, quoted in Welch, 1982, p. 19). Teresa compares this state to a larva in its cocoon, before it is reborn as a butterfly. It symbolizes the soul dying in Christ and rising to a transformed life.

In the sixth place there is an intensified union with God. Teresa invites the soul to open to a mystical experience, which she experienced in the form of a betrothal and time of cleansing as a necessary prerequisite for the spiritual marriage that occurs in the next dwelling place. The experience of God is likened to a fire in the heart. The soul feels the pain of wounds in its depths and at the same time release from the pain like the removal of an arrow from the heart. Pain and joy are equally intense. Union with God affects body, mind, and imagination powerfully, requiring a courageous response.

In the seventh dwelling place the intensified union with God becomes complete. Teresa relates an intellectual understanding of the Holy Trinity and its lasting awareness in the heart. The union with Christ culminates in what she calls spiritual marriage. It is a very deep interior experience that cannot be adequately described in words. The soul becomes one with God. The analogy of rainwater falling in a river best describes her experience. She also likens the union to the joining of two wax candles, making the flame, wax, and wick of the two into one and the same. It is like a stream running into the sea. It is an experience of inseparableness. The experience leads to an interior peace and a desire to suffer for God. The inner dryness in prayer or inner disturbance experienced in the sixth place disappears producing an extraordinary calm and quiet.

Teresa's journey of prayer mainly consists of the mental imagery mode. Elaborate descriptions of the Interior Castle with its many mansions and the kind of attitudes and efforts undertaken by the soul can capture the mind and heart of the contemplative. Articles of faith are pictorially portrayed, and spiritual progress is made in stages. We see how Teresa employs the imagination only to transcend it in order to be receptive to what is freely given. One can identify the two very different functions of the cerebral hemispheres. The key, as Teresa points out, is not to think. She does not actually describe the steps for vocal and discursive prayers. But we can infer that vocal prayer means simply speaking to God, and discursive meditation is focusing on themes of faith such as the Holy Trinity, the lives of the saints, or scenes from the gospels, and so on. All of these forms of prayer are just a beginning. Teresa then moves from active prayer to a contemplative prayer of quiet and union. Again, she insists on being merely passive because what happens in advanced contemplation does not result from human ingenuity but divine gratuity.

St . John of the Cross

St. John of the Cross was a contemporary of St. Teresa. He also contributed to the mystical tradition extensively, but his works are much more complex. Mental imagery is used heavily earlier in his works only to be completely abandoned later. One of his classics, The Ascent of Mount Carmel: The Dark Night, describes a path to perfection in which the soul enters into a union of love with God. He proposes a systematic rationale for aspirants of mystical spirituality. He illustrates how after having gone through active and passive purifications the soul is able to enjoy a state of absolute union with the divine Bridegroom. It is a journey of the soul through the "dark night" which leads ultimately to the mount of perfection. The reason that the night is dark is because it involves 1) a mortification of the appetites, 2) a journey of faith, and 3) God's communication to the soul. All of them transcend the sensory and imagery modes.

The soul consists of two parts: sensory and spiritual. The sensory has interior and exterior categories. The five senses of seeing, hearing, smelling, tasting, and touching are the sensory exterior components. Fantasy and imagination are the inner components. The spiritual consists of three faculties: intellect, memory, and will. Intellect and memory belong to both the sensory and spiritual parts. Before union with God, the soul must pass through two principal kinds of nights during which the two parts of the soul must undergo purgation or purification. The dual manner with which purification of the soul can occur is: actively, through its own efforts; or passively, through the grace of God without human effort.

1.) Mortification of the Appetites

According to John the very theme of Ascent is the mortification of the appetites. The metaphor "dark night" signifies the idea of deprivation. The love experience of the soul is negative in the sense that according to John to love is to "deprive oneself for God of all that is not God" (Kavanaugh & Rodriguez, 1979, p. 46). Night itself is privation of light and all objects made visible by light. Mortification of the appetites is a dark night for the soul. "To deprive oneself of the gratification of the appetites in all things is like living in darkness and in a void" (pp. 46-48). John substitutes the word "appetites" for "attachment, affection, the love of creatures, the will for something, inclination, and desire" (p. 48). Privation seems negative but it is meant for a positive purpose. All appetites of both the sensory and the spiritual must be directed towards God instead of worldly objects.

The soul must deny and mortify gratification derived from the five senses: hearing, sight, smell, taste, and touch, and empty the mind of its images. What John calls for is to move beyond sensations and mental imagery to become completely passive in order to receive what is freely granted by God. Anything that can arise through human emotions and intelligence does not compare to what is truly divine. In fact, what we experience through mind and body appears to be in contrast to that freely granted by God. Our sensual pleasure and appeasement are "intense suffering, torment, and bitterness for God" (Kavanaugh & Larkin, 1987, p. 68). Tainted by the pleasures of life, the soul becomes like a smudgy window unable to allow the light to come to illuminate a room.

How should one enter this part of the night? It is done actively in the initial stage or later passively. For the active form, John sketches a journey to a summit in the form of a mount and on it writes short verses that need to be repeated in the sensory or imagery mode. A person repeats these verses in order to climb the mountain. Some of the verses that are powerfully paradoxical are worthy of mention.

> To reach satisfaction in all, desire its possession in nothing; to come to the knowledge of all, desire the knowledge of nothing; to come to possess all, desire the possession of nothing; to come to the pleasure you have not, you must go by a way in which you enjoy not; to come to the possession you have not, you must go by a way in which you possess not; to come to be what you are not, you must go by a way in which you are not; and when you come to the possession of all, you must possess it without wanting anything; and lastly, nothing, nothing, nothing, nothing, nothing, nothing and even on the Mount nothing (Kavanaugh & Larkin, 1987, p. 45, quoted in Amalraj, 2002, Figure Example 15).

Each sentence contains the wisdom of the mystical journey. Next, John elaborates how to receive passively what is given by God in the third section which discusses the communication of God.

2) The Journey of Faith

John compares the first part of the night, in which mortification of the appetites and denial of sense pleasures occur, to twilight, during which sensory objects grow fainter. This part, known as the journey of faith, is likened to midnight in which the night becomes much darker than the previous part. The third part of the night, when the soul receives communication from God, is compared to the period before dawn that precedes the illumination of the day. Daytime itself is likened to the divine rays of enlightenment.

Faith is necessary for the soul's union with God. What seems special about John's view is that he distinguishes faith from intellect. There is faith that is independent of intelligence. On its own, intellect is incapable of acquiring knowledge of the supernatural mysteries of God. By faith, John means an "obscure encounter" with God (Kavanaugh & Rodriguez, 1979, p. 51). To enter into such a union with God, "one must lean on faith, take it for his guide and light, and rest on nothing of what he understands, tastes, feels, or imagines" (p. 51). John expects the aspirant to rid himself of all that is related to the senses and even imagination of sensation. The journey is unquestionably stalled when one is "attached to any understanding, feeling, imagining, opinion, will or way of his own, or to any other of his works or affairs" (Kavanaugh & Larkin, 1987, p. 51). It is a complete departure from a thinking mind and feeling body. Is there faith independent of reason? The answer is yes, according to John.

John speaks of two interior bodily senses: imagination and fantasy. Imagination means bringing before the mind's eyes sense realities. Fantasy adds color to more imaginative pictures. Both produce images and figures. Meditation is the work of these two faculties. John invites the practitioner to let go of even good discursive meditation that centers on "imagining of Christ crucified;" God seated upon a glorious throne in majesty and splendor and light; or focusing the mind on any human or divine object imaginable. The soul must deny these images and leave the senses and mental imagery in darkness for the divine union. It is necessary that one learn to abide in "that quietude with a loving attentiveness to God" (Kavanaugh & Larkin, 1987, p. 139). Faculties cannot receive anything from God actively but rather only passively. At this stage faith becomes love for John.

3) The Dark Night and the Communication of God

The ascent itself is a journey of the soul to reach the mount of perfection by choosing to mortify its appetites and hold on to nothing but pure faith. The Night, on the other hand, stands for what God does by purifying the soul and letting it passively receive, bringing faith and love to perfection. The communication from God is twofold. Divine life is communicated through the senses and its images initially, but increasingly God leads the soul to receive more spiritual communication without the aid of the senses. John uses various terms to identify communication from God: "inflow, infusion, manifestation, illustration, illumination," and so forth (Kavanaugh & Larkin, 1987, p. 56).

What is granted by God through the senses is compared to morsels, but the inflow that enters the soul passively is a feast beyond depiction. In the last part of the passive night, God communicates general and obscure knowledge by infusion. This passive purification is said to be "painful" rather than delightful to the soul. John recounts the results of God's communication to the soul variously: God demonstrates to the soul its miserable state; abandonment by God and creatures becomes painful to bear; the soul suffers terrible apathy and feels as if being confined to a dungeon, "bound hands and feet, and able neither to move, nor see, nor feel any favor from heaven or earth" (p. 56); there is continuation of torment; and finally there arises an intense hunger and thirst for God by disposing it to withdraw from any appetite for any object (p. 57). God dries the soul of all its desires before it is "capable of receiving light, warmth, strength, and plenitude of God's grace" (Kavanaugh & Larkin, 1987, pp. 58-59). Thus union with God occurs negatively by the denial of all that is desirable in earthly life. After all human efforts have been made, communication from God further purifies the soul in dark experiences such as helplessness and abandonment before the union occurs gratuitously.

The mystical journey begins more in the analytical part of the left brain. Eventually, it moves on to the right hemisphere that is able to quiet its counterpart. But when faith enters in, it does away with all mental and sensory efforts. Faith, according to John, is dissociated from intelligence. It is simply a loving gaze on God. At this point in the journey, faith becomes love and faith itself perhaps disappears. One abides in love to experience an overflow of love that comes into the soul more in the pains rather than the delights of life. The experience of paradox is beyond the capability of either hemisphere. Certainly, the journey has a definite cerebral beginning, but intelligence is most assuredly transcends it when God steps in.

Implications for Insightful Scriptural Reflections

Thus we have an insightful background for the prayer methods of the mystics. Today's medical science and transpersonal psychology have verified a significant impact of contemplative meditation on body, mind, and spirit. The measurable impact of these prayers can be experienced in how they lead to a sense of relaxation and calm which occurs naturally. Surprisingly, these practices guide a person to deeper layers of love and peace which are spontaneous and intrinsic. So great is the transformation that one learns to pair opposites and be comfortable with the paradox. What you do not understand need not concern you any more than what you do understand. What you cannot control need not make you feel any less capable. When you are weak, you can feel strong. When you are insulted and oppressed, you have the freedom to rejoice. You are blessed even when you suffer hunger and poverty. You can bless those who curse you. You can offer the other cheek without becoming angry or retaliatory. You can forgive freely without requiring an apology because forgiveness from God is freely given.

The following chapter will present a series of reflections that you will experience as you continue to persevere in contemplative meditation. Prayerful union with God will enable you to see the opposite of things when you experience something that is painful and dehumanizing. Years of contemplative prayer will enable you to become inspired by God's word. Whatever you have been disagreeing with can become a matter of harmony. The old suddenly will become new. You resolve the problem from within and not from without. Changing oneself in small measure is totally different from completely being transformed from within by divine grace. Forgiveness is something you do not gain but is always given freely for those who believe. If God's love is unconditional, forgiveness is a part of that package. You are free when you fall into God's hands.

Chapter IV

A word of caution

People use meditation for a variety of purposes: to pray, focus, heal, de-stress, relax, concentrate, and become mindful. Physical and mental exercises that precede prayer generally involve abdominal breathing and flexing and relaxing of muscles. In the process large quantities of oxygen are pumped in as food for the brain. Two branches of the nervous system undergo a sense of calm. The goal of the practice in this book is spiritual growth. How do I learn not to be anxious so as to experience the unconditional love that is already in me? How do I surrender to the love of God that is always being poured upon me? One needs to be receptive to the greatest love that embraces the individual, regardless of his/her state. It is a state of being in communion with that love that has nothing to do with earning or performing or deserving. Deep faith is the greatest action. Faith and action become intertwined. Faith is action and action is faith.

Linda Wasmer Andrews (2005) writes about health, the mind/ body connection, and psychology. In her book Stress Control: For Peace of Mind, she explains how to use meditation for spiritual growth. People who practice meditation begin first with some "focused deep breathing" in order to get into a "calm and receptive frame of mind" (p. 43). As I have indicated in previous chapters, the right hemisphere of the brain can be readied to receive a more comprehensive understanding than mere rational knowledge. "While still in the meditative state, they [practitioners of meditation] reflect on a certain experience, issue, or spiritual truth in order to gain greater insight into it" says Andrews (2005, p. 43-44). The deeper the meditation, the greater is the inspiration. Knowledge deduced by the left hemisphere is different from the wisdom generated by the right hemisphere. People gain insights that are much deeper than the knowledge typical of the right-brain thinking. In a deep state of contemplative meditation meaning may be completely transformed from being simply intellectual knowledge to wisdom, which is the embodiment of inspiration.

The following section contains a series of scripture passages drawn from daily and Sunday liturgy with references to chapters and verses and lectionary numbers under the title. The topics themselves are as paradoxical as the wisdom that inspired these reflections. It is important that you read the relevant scripture passages slowly and meditatively before you read the commentary. Otherwise it might be hard to relate to the message. You may miss the essence of the passage. Hours of contemplative meditation have preceded these reflections. When you read the commentary reflectively you may run into problems. It is likely that some may find them at times objectionable, annoying, irritating, or disagreeable. These feelings are understandable because we tend to think through issues in a linear and logical way rather than in a contemplative manner.

Correct logic and perfect performance alone do not and cannot resolve the problems of life. Solutions lie beyond our understanding and control. It is not so much a matter of how to understand as how to surrender and trust without understanding or explanation. After all, Jesus was challenged by some of the most brilliant minds, the most educated of the Jews, the Pharisees and scribes, who knew the law. But despite being experts in the Mosaic Law, they could not fathom the deepest love of God. Some twenty years ago, I would have objected to what I am saying now. I disagreed with this notion only to find myself accepting it later. The rational mind still cannot comprehend why Jesus says: "Blessed are you who are poor, for the kingdom of God is yours. Blessed are you who are now hungry, for you will be satisfied. Blessed are you who are now weeping, for you will laugh" (Lk 6: 20, 21). "Blessed are they who are persecuted for the sake of the righteousness, for theirs is the kingdom of heaven. Blessed are you when they insult you and persecute you and utter every kind of evil against you [falsely] because of me. Rejoice and be glad, for your reward will be great in heaven" (Mt 5: 10, 11). Jesus promises to reverse the injustices of this world in the hereafter, and he calls upon us to trust and rejoice even as conditions remain unchanged in the here and now. Paradox is understood only over a period of time in life's journey. What does not make sense today will gradually become clear as we age and mature. It is with that sense of hope I invite you to read and enjoy the wisdom that has transformed me.

It is not about doing it right

Luke 15: 1-10 (# 488)

Our spiritual life may not merely be about doing it right or correctly as it is often preached to us. Doing it right alone does not make us righteous. Conformity to external rules is not everything. It is only a minimum. Observing laws exactly the way prescribed will not make us holy. It may lead to self-justification or entitlement. Justification is something given to us as a free gift and is never earned. It is not a reward for a moral life.

Paul lived the life of a Pharisee and followed every law faithfully. He called himself the stock of Israel and a Hebrew of the Hebrews. In his earnestness to be righteous he was zealous in legal observance and a flawless observer of the law. He claimed himself to be above reproach in matters related to justice based on law (Phil 3: 3-8). In doing everything right he was wrong because he ended up persecuting the Church.

It is possible for us to do everything correctly hoping to acquire a right relationship with God. Many times it may have been based on fear of punishment, guilt or shame, or hope for reward. Pharisees interpreted a good life as a reward for perfect observance of the law and the life of suffering as a punishment for sin. A God extravagantly offering forgiveness even to a prodigal son may not have been possible in their conception of God. No wonder they were very judgmental of themselves and others. Their observance may have centered on any of the above mentioned causes. In their desire to adhere to perfectionism, they did exactly what was required, but no more, even though they were capable of doing so. God was probably perceived as punishing and extremely demanding. The concept of a God being lavishly merciful and forgiving may not have captured their attention as much as a God who expected everything to be done right. The Kingdom of God was a reward the Pharisees thought they earned for living right. Maybe they were not terribly sinful human beings, but being right alone did not justify them before God. What they failed to perceive was that God was willing to forgive them even if they failed to observe the law. Because they indulged in right observances they did not think they needed the mercy of God like other sinners such as the tax collectors, prostitutes, and the unchurched. So they did not associate with the sinners because they perceived them as deserving God's punishment and unworthy of God's Kingdom. They did not recognize their own need for repentance and forgiveness because they followed the letter of the law perfectly.

Humbled by being labeled as sinners, the not-so-law-abiding acknowledged their need for the mercy and forgiveness of God. They heard Jesus reveal the exceptional love of God expressed in terms of seeking the lost (Lk 15: 1-10). Contrary to the image of an unapproachable and fearful God, Jesus revealed a loving God searching for one lost sheep, leaving behind the ninety-nine that had not lost their way. The righteous did not feel the need to repent but the lost ones did. The more the lost ones needed God, the more God was offering himself freely. The more the righteous did not think they needed God's mercy, the more they restricted His coming into their lives. Nor could they imagine a God who would be in search of sinners to offer them His boundless mercy rather than bestowing rewards to the self-righteous.

You will be hated because of my name: love your enemies

Luke 21: 5-11 (# 504)

The Jerusalem temple was the center of Jewish pride, honor, and hope as God's dwelling. Jews could not envision its destruction. When it did happen, it appeared to indicate the end of the world. For Jesus' contemporaries it might have indicated his second coming. Yet the delay of his return raised more questions than answers. The persecution that followed baffled early Christians.

Jesus himself predicted the temple that looked so wonderful would not be left one stone upon another. One could expect some kind of a warning before it happened. Jesus talked about many other signs that might be interpreted as warnings. Many would claim to be him returning. Wars and insurrections would occur. But the end would not be near. Cataclysmic wars, seismic catastrophes, epidemics, starvation, and ominous displays in the sky could possibly be signs of the end. Worse would be persecution. Individuals would be betrayed by parents, brothers, sisters, relatives, and friends. People would be brought before governors and kings before being thrown into prisons to be tortured and persecuted and even put to death. "You will be hated by all because of my name" (Lk 21:17).

Yet the believers were asked not be concerned about how to defend themselves with words or actions. Jesus asked them to be unarmed and defenseless. He promised words and wisdom that would dumbfound the adversaries. Not a hair of their heads would be destroyed. By patient perseverance, the believers were to save their lives.

All the incidents of the gospel passage suggest how Luke recalled the words of Jesus to explain the destruction of the Jerusalem temple, the delay of Jesus' return, and the unstoppable persecution in which believers paid the ultimate price for their faith. Yet the vindication Jesus promises does not seem to be related to material evils alone. "Fear not" are the words addressed to them, yet there is no escape from torture and death. Believers are asked not to fear anything, and ironically they remain unprotected and abandoned. It seems paradoxical. Jesus promises a vindication beyond death, a justification after death, which needs to be accepted in faith and trust even during life and death.

The terrorists who razed the Twin Towers in New York killed almost 3,000 people. Innocent and good people died unjust, unfair, and violent deaths. They did not deserve such a tragic fate. Terrorists who committed the atrocity claimed to be martyrs who would marry seventy-two virgins in heaven. Christ commands his disciples to show the other cheek when struck on one. Love your enemies, bless those who curse you, and pray for those who persecute you. Jesus never commands revenge against one's enemies. If you do not fight those who fight you and suffer an unjust and violent death, you are a martyr who will be vindicated after death. Indeed, all those lives that were lost are martyrs but ironically not the terrorists!

In spite of faith, believers will experience injustice from which they are promised to be redeemed beyond death. To face such a dilemma and still believe requires not ordinary faith but extraordinary. What is guaranteed is not an immediate solution always, but justification beyond the unfairness. Irresolvable conditions then can be seized as opportunities to deepen faith and trust in God rather than being perceived as signs of abandonment or neglect.

The blind man was spiritually able to see Jesus even before being restored

Luke 18: 35-43 (# 497)

Jesus was on his way to Jerusalem where he would fulfill the predictions of his suffering, death, and resurrection. He challenged the crowd to follow him closely, warning that it would cost them. To follow in his footsteps, deeper faith would be required.

There are characters who would respond to his appeal. One of them was the blind man (Lk 18: 35-43). He did not see Jesus nor did he talk to him. Perhaps he must have heard people speak of him as one doing great things. Some might have told him that he was one of the great prophets or the Messiah, the Redeemer. Due to his lack of eyesight to verify these things, he must have taken pieces of information to his heart. Through the eye of his soul, he simply believed what the crowd journeying with him with eyes open failed to see: Jesus as the Son of God, a solution to all human problems. How could they not see him? He saw Jesus in his heart, requiring no evidence for his belief.

No one could stop the blind man from being able to see Jesus in his heart. In his heart he knew that Jesus was merciful and compassionate. He was not born a sinner because God had condemned him as the Pharisees said. He did not deserve to be born blind and did not and could not understand why. Even if he had committed a terrible sin, he still believed he deserved God's mercy. So he begged for pity and sympathy. What he looked for was mercy, but what was granted to him was righteousness that the Pharisees claimed for themselves and denied him. He knew he could not justify himself but only God could, even though he remained a sinner. It was just an unearned and undeserved gift.

His request was for more than physical recovery. He knew he had a much greater need than receiving his eyesight. When he was in God's presence, nothing could prevent him from seeing God. There should not and cannot be any other physical or emotional need if he is with God. To be in God's Kingdom was to be freed from all wants. He knew that he did not need eyes to believe Jesus was the Son of David. What he asked for was spiritual healing, a union of his soul with God. He desired to be with God who appeared to him in human form. Much more than his own recovery, he desired to see the miracle that Jesus was, God walking in the person of Jesus.

His expectations were beyond his body and mind. When Jesus asked the blind man what he wanted, he called Jesus "Lord," a title that would be given to Jesus after his resurrection. He went past the mysteries of the suffering, death, and resurrection of Jesus. He knew that Jesus would live beyond those mortal realities. He expressed that to have vision did not mean just the ability to see with the eyes. He desired to be with the Lord. He was so advanced in his spiritual journey, unlike many who remained at a spiritual distance from Jesus although they traveled closely with him. Without further adieu, Jesus restored the blind man's sight and pointed out that his faith had made the miracle inevitable. His faith was the miracle. After the healing there were no directions given to the man because Jesus then became his only direction. Because he intended to be with the Lord, not just merely see him, he followed Jesus on his journey. He had no other priority more important than to be with the Lord who was a great miracle to follow and admire. The blind man opened the eyes of everyone who claimed to see Jesus and taught the followers about discipleship required to truly see Jesus. He discovered a reason for his sight: to give glory to God. He received the highest level of healing unlike many who sought and received only physical and emotional recovery, but remained spiritually blind. Miracles need not necessarily lead to deeper faith because even a blind man can see Jesus, "for we walk by faith, not by sight" (2 Cor 5:7).

More will be given to the one who has more

Luke 19: 11-28 (# 499)

Jesus was nearing his long journey to Jerusalem. His contemporaries believed that the Kingdom of God would appear there. The Kingdom was thought to be more a materialistic existence that would bring death to enemies of God, the lawless, and the untouchables. By observing the law the Pharisees, the Scribes, and the leaders of Israel believed they were entitled to the Kingdom of God here on earth. For Jesus, a mere mechanical observation of externals did not warrant anyone the Kingdom, if the observances had not been internalized, taken to heart. Only deeper faith in God that came both as a challenge and a blessing in the person of Jesus would pave the way to acknowledge the Kingdom as a gift rather than a prerogative.

To underscore how important it was to believe the gift that was being offered to them in the person of Jesus, he told his followers the following parable. A noble man went away to a distant country entrusting ten of his servants with ten gold coins each, instructing them to invest them until he came back (Lk 19: 11-28). Though all received equal amounts of money, one doubled his money and another earned half of what was lent. A third did not multiply the riches but buried the coins because he considered the noble man harsh.

Curiosity is increased when one examines what Jesus could have meant by "wealth" and "the expected revenue" in this parable. Presumably, they stand for talents and gifts and their duplication. But this may lead to a mere literal understanding of the gospel. The money may have represented the Law and faith, its necessary multiplication, which should have developed due to its preserved practice. While the Mosaic Law multiplied into many other laws, faith did not increase proportionately. The doubling of revenue meant those full-fledged in faith did more than what was required, multiplying the capital and its profits. The religious leaders kept themselves to a mere mechanical repetition of laws. Duplication of laws did not correspond to proportionate augmentation of faith.

Whereas some people progressed in their faith and trust in God by transcending the laws, others were stuck. Interestingly, Jesus further develops the situation of the servant who buried his master's money. The reason the servant perceived the master to be a harsh man was because, as he said, "you take up what you did not lay down and you harvest what you did not plant" (Lk 19: 21). The master was upset because the servant did not deposit the money in the bank even though he claimed he feared him. Even if the dread of God was the motivation for observance of the law, if accurately and sincerely followed, it would have yielded some benefits. But external observance of the law was in vain. Even the mere repetition was ineffective.

The one who followed the law and did more than what was expected had grown deeply in faith leading to greater understanding of God. The one who did not even repeat it sincerely forfeited all opportunities to advance in faith. All that potential would now belong to the one who had already exercised his faith and would discover even greater love. Those who rejected God's Son would recognize how much resistance they held against God. The Son was the replacement for the law. Whereas most preferred following the letter of the law, the Son invited them into a relationship with the divine. Even the apparent faith they claimed in observing externals would disappear because the externals had failed to mean what the rituals and symbols signified. As the people's practices were empty, they would embrace nothingness by losing even the apparent meaning of the rituals. What they did not seek on earth they would not find in heaven.

The criminal who believed in God dying by his side

Luke 23: 35-43 (# 163)

Jesus was hanging on the cross. Although he had the power to walk away from the cross, he was silent and unopposing in his final battle. An innocent person was being violated; a just man was being unjustly punished. The righteous did not deserve to die in such a way. The Son of God who called himself Son of Man was abandoned by his heavenly Father. The living God's only Son was dying. The God of life allowed death to overcome his Son. Although obedience was optional, Jesus chose to surrender so that God could transform him. The way of glory was through the way of the cross, resisting temptations to redeem in a way that was not God's way.

As the people stood by and watched Jesus hanging on the cross, religious leaders mocked Jesus saying that he had saved others and should save himself if he were truly the Messiah. The soldiers challenged him to save himself, if he were the King of the Jews. There was an inscription on the cross, "This is the King of the Jews." One of the criminals cursed and told Jesus to save himself and them, if Jesus were the Messiah. Everyone around Jesus challenged him to come down from the cross miraculously and prove that he was the Son of God and they would then believe him. This was the temptation Jesus resolutely avoided from the very beginning of his public ministry. Led to the desert by the Spirit of God, Jesus fasted for forty days and nights. While the tempter suggested to Jesus to have his own way rather than abiding by the way of his Father, Jesus continuously resisted the attraction to follow his own way and submitted himself to the Father out of obedience. The climax of that obedience was the crucifixion.

It seemed evident that Jesus was after all not the Son of God. If he were, he would not be dying defenselessly on the cross because he would have been saved by his God. Everything portrayed helplessness and rejection. He appeared to be someone who claimed to be God's Son, but badly disappointed.

There was one person who thought of the reality differently. That was the good criminal. He knew he deserved to die, as did his compatriot, because of the crimes they had committed. When the other thief cursed Jesus, the good thief calmed him down by saying that they had earned their punishment but Jesus had not. Looking at the bloody figure of Jesus hanging on the cross beside him, the good thief believed that Jesus was innocent and was dying unjustly. The one next to him was the God who allowed injustice, an unjustifiable punishment to be exacted by humans. He also knew that death could not destroy Jesus but that he would ultimately overcome death and return to his heavenly kingdom. He believed not only that evil could not annihilate the innocent and just, but also that the good would be victorious in the end. Even though the world condemned him to die, he believed he could be reconciled to God in the eleventh hour. Therefore he made the most moving statement of faith, "Jesus, remember me when you come into your kingdom."

This sentence has become the oft-repeated prayer mantra of saints and mystics. As he saw Jesus unjustly punished, he could recognize God in Jesus and believe that he would be forgiven by a merciful God even as the world condemned him to die. He knew that in God's heart there was always forgiveness, even moments before one's death. He also taught believers the way to receive mercy. He simply trusted that God would forgive if he merely asked for forgiveness. It is a gift freely given even to the undeserved. The criminal was challenged to believe that the wrongly condemned person dying next to him was God. Furthermore, to believe in mercy from a dying God when the whole world refused to show pity is all the more an expression of faith. Pardon is unmerited and always offered because of faith in the ever-forgiving God. To believe that he was not being rejected by God even when the humans passed judgment on him was an expression of extraordinary faith.

A Gentile had more faith than all of Israel

Matthew 8: 5-11 (# 176)

A centurion in Capernaum approached Jesus and pleaded with Jesus to cure his servant who was paralyzed and seriously ill. He was a man of authority under whom served many soldiers and civilians. He also was conscious of his authority and its power. His command was communicated in words which were translated into realities immediately. This man did not seem to have abused his authority nor was he harsh with his servants. He was genuinely concerned about his servants and their well-being. If not, he would not have been worried about the dying servant.

Another trait of this centurion must have been humility. For this reason, he decided to approach Jesus himself rather than sending word through another. He must have been personally interested in his ill servant. In his heart he strongly believed that the man called Jesus was God. Alien to Judaism, he simply believed that Jesus, who appeared in the human form, was indeed God. He also knew in his heart that Jesus had authority over all creation. Jesus had the absolute power over disease and death.

When Jesus offered to come and cure his servant, the centurion did not think he deserved to receive him in his home because he was a Gentile. Jews did not visit the homes of the Gentiles. He did not feel that he was worthy to welcome Jesus. But he also did not believe that Jesus would refuse to enter his home simply because he was a Gentile. But Jesus was busy teaching and preaching. Besides, the job could be done from a distance. He knew what it was to give orders and get things done from a distance. Word of his command generated power and was translated into reality. He knew he had control over many mundane things.

Somehow in his heart the centurion knew that Jesus had absolute control over life and death because Jesus was God. Rather than troubling himself to come down and cure him, Jesus could just give the command and his servant would be healed. Jesus was amazed at the expression of faith of a centurion who was unschooled in Judaism. The commander resembled Abraham in his faith and trust. Jesus could not but appreciate him. He was a model of many who would come from the east and the west and recline at table with Abraham, Isaac, and Jacob in the Kingdom of heaven. Jesus predicted a way of entering into heaven through means other than just being religious.

Being religious may or may not necessarily be spiritual. Although they both ideally should coexist, one can exist without the other. If it must be, it is better to be spiritual than religious because many claimed to be devoutly religious but in fact were not spiritual and, therefore, far removed from God's kingdom. Prostitutes and sinners who were irreligious were justified and made spiritual by Jesus. What is suggested is that entry is made through the heart rather than through the head; total surrender as opposed to a mechanical compliance to externals. In fact, learning to operate from the heart will demand more than what the head dictates. Relationship with God will defy logic and rationality. Love through knowing is feasible as humans, but "love of the unknowing" is required for a journey with God. Love through knowing is conditional and defensive but love through unknowing is unconditional and risky. While the former is human, the latter can be human and divine. The greater the risk-taking, the deeper will be the level of love. To journey with God, one has to learn to walk the unknown without fear. "Even though I walk through a dark valley I fear no harm" will be personally meaningful.

Judge not and you will not be judged

Matthew 3: 1-12 (# 4)

John the Baptist preached in the desert, "Repent, for the kingdom of heaven is at hand." What Isaiah foretold regarding the second liberation from Babylon was meant to be a message of encouragement and hope to the exiles during slavery (Is 40: 3). A path was to be prepared for the intervention of God to lead people out of bondage. It was indeed a prefiguration of God's long promised Messiah, not a political liberator as the Jews had expected. Matthew's description of the Baptist's attire was what had been worn by the Prophet Elijah (2 Kings 1: 8) who was supposed to return before the day of the Lord (Mal 3: 23).

For 400 years there were no prophets in Israel, and John claimed to herald the coming of the Messiah and proclaimed the message of repentance. To the Jews, the baptism of repentance was inconceivable since it was meant only for the sinful Gentiles before reception into the chosen people. Through blood ties to Abraham, all the descendents were guaranteed the kingdom if they merely followed the Law. Major events of their personal and national history were attributed to the treasury merits earned by Father Abraham. While the uneducated did receive baptism of repentance, the elite, the Pharisees and the Sadducees, went to judge John, proclaiming the ritual unnecessary. Because they came to judge his actions, they were being judged by John.

John the Baptist proclaimed that the wrath and judgment of God awaited the elite since they were presumptuous. Rather than reflecting the faith of Abraham they believed their physical affinity to him was alone sufficient for reception into God's Kingdom. They came to a virtual standstill in goodness because of their compliance to mere external observations of the law without personalization. Where had they made their mistake? Why was repentance difficult? What was/is meant by repentance?

When John invited the people of Israel to repentance, it was not to a mere feeling of remorse and acknowledgment of guilt and shame over the wrong. It included these feelings, of course, but was much more. What underlies the need for repentance is a sense of lack of open-mindedness.

Failing to be unbiased, unprejudiced, nonjudgmental, and sensitive left them stuck in stubborn, opinionated, lopsided, arrogant, egotistical, and self-righteous ways. These characteristics allow any person in any time to become a Pharisee. This psychological make-up speaks volumes more to personality traits than to historical roles. The stronger the resistance, the harsher the message directed to them.

To accept John as the forerunner of the Messiah and to welcome him meant extraordinary open-mindedness, such as that of a child. Faith demanded more than the Law. While observance of the law required only a minimum, faith would desire more than the maximum. While observance of law perceives only a conditional love, faith will enable one to embrace unconditional love. The greater the level of faith, the greater is the perception of love. Faith is to believe in the impossible. When Isaiah promised the ideal king, a new shoot from the root of Jesse, he portrayed the impossible conditions: a wolf at peace with a lamb; a lion in concord with an ox; and a child playing with a cobra (Is 11: 1-10). It was not a mere geopolitical restoration, but the re-creation of the Garden of Eden when the Kingdom would become fully realized. Humility and open- mindedness lead to a nonjudgmental attitude whereby we become repentant. When we become judgmental we are unrepentant, and therefore we will be judged for being who we are. The Judge will only let us see how we judged ourselves.

In reflecting on the necessity of the open-mindedness required to experience unconditional love, it amazes me how some Icelanders welcome even winter blues. They do not suffer the usual winter blues people in other parts undergo. They consider winter depression as "a powerful creator…. You can be very happy even when you're depressed. Laughing people aren't necessarily happy, and a crying man is not necessarily sad" said a well-known writer and thinker Gunnar Dal (The New York Times). Being unprejudiced enables one to experience love in depression and anxiety because love is never excluded from any human experience.

The invisible is present in the visible

Mark 4: 26-34 (# 321)

We are used to physical, emotional, and intellectual realities. It is hard to imagine spiritual realities such as our soul, heaven, angels, saints, and God. But these are as real as our mundane existence. Jesus reduces the higher truths to mere happenings of nature. The farmer can feel the seeds in his hands, plant them in the ground, water them, and just wait for the shoots to sprout. These visible realities do not demonstrate how growth occurs invisibly. Tangible reality reaches its climax when it is ready for harvest. Jesus compares the unknowable growth of the seed to the plant. Something of it is seen but something of it is unseen and yet proven by its sprouting. For the early Christian community that struggled to understand not only how the Messiah could die on the cross after he proclaimed the inauguration of the Kingdom of God, but also why he did not return to free people from persecution as he had promised, may have been fundamental to Mark's recollection of Jesus' words. His idea may have been to point out the "already and not yet" component of the Kingdom.

As people experienced the overriding of an earthly kingdom and its rampage through persecution of the Kingdom initiated by Jesus, it must have been hard to continue to believe that his Kingdom was already in existence because of the human tragedies that had come to pass. The challenge to the early community was to acknowledge that their passion and suffering did not negate the presence of the Kingdom, but rather entitled them to enter into heaven here on earth even as they suffered. Their passion was in fact a prerequisite to that entry. Their hope centered on the words of Jesus promising a definite harvest: the end of the time of evil. There was no easy and immediate remedy guaranteed.

It appears that Jesus had a problem presenting images to compare to the birth of the Kingdom. It is an example of how hard it is to explain it and how much harder it is to believe in its presence after the hearing. Jesus moves on to present another analogy: the mustard seed. He juxtaposes two superlatives: the smallest versus the biggest. The smallest seed grows into the largest plant. The microcosm will certainly develop into a macrocosm. The present times do not seem to offer any clue to the presence or growth of the Kingdom. The rise and fall of many kingdoms are part of human history.

Due to their visibility and tangibility, history records their stories. Jesus invites the audience to imagine the invisible unfolding of it every day. We are called to live it every day as if we had seen it with the naked eye. Saints and mystics appear to be more conscious of the invisible realities than the visible. The visible seem to be merely symbolic of the supernatural.

St. Francis of Assisi was moved to tears after looking at the sunset for a while because in the beauty of creation he saw the Creator. He fell in love with creation and composed a poem The Canticle of the Sun. He loved to address creation as Sister Moon and the stars, Brother Wind, Sister Water, Mother Earth, and even Sister Bodily Death. Immaterial beings became animated beings that reflected God.

The words of Jesus are much more a challenge than a problem. Heeding his words requires a whole different attitude toward our life. Since the Kingdom has been initiated and moves on to its fullest revelation, we have the option of entering into heaven while we live here on earth. Can I live my life as if I were already in heaven with compassion, charity, kindness, forgiveness, mercy, and gratitude? Can I not live my hell on earth by being arrogant, insensitive, and refusing to forgive? Whatever we build on earth will concurrently be set in heaven. Neither heaven nor hell is a surprise because we have already been gifted to choose them here and now.

Blessed are the poor and the not so poor

Matthew 5: 1-12 (# 71)

Our priorities in life are in striking contrast to God's plan. The definition of self-worth is drawn from what we possess, achieve, hold, or have as opposed to accepting ourselves as we are. Therefore losses, grief, failures, adversities, brokenness, anxiety, or depression are seemingly worthless. In God's dictionary this is reversed. Mingling with and often found in the company of the downtrodden and scum of the society, Jesus invited them to rejoice. His contemporaries, like ours, considered good fortune, healthy children, and reputation in the society to be blessings. Lack of these material blessings was considered suffering which was a result of sin. Jesus proclaimed an opposite message calling the poor, the suffering and sorrowing "blessed."

As Luke's gospel proclaimed, "Blessed are you who are poor" (6: 20), Matthew's words echoed, "Blessed are the poor in spirit" (5: 3). Mere poverty does not entitle one to God's Kingdom. Poverty can also breed murder, terrorism, violence, selfishness, and greed. Lack of material blessings does not dehumanize one as much as the emotional estimate of it as abandonment or worthlessness before humans and God. Ironically, a poor person is challenged to consider himself invaluable in the eyes of God who makes the poor rich by his unfailing presence in them. Sending forth his disciples to proclaim the Kingdom, Jesus exhorted them to bring nothing with them. They were asked to embrace poverty voluntarily to experience the providence of God.

Poverty can be a prerequisite to experiencing the abundance of God. If lack of possessions can become the means to interiorize poverty, then the not-so-poor can follow the same path toward total dependence on God. Instead of viewing one's worth in terms of possessions, power, intelligence, influence, beauty, success, health, or reputation, a person can hold himself priceless without any of these because of God's unconditional presence. In fact, rich or poor, healthy or unhealthy, young or old, strong or weak, guilty or innocent, and right or wrong does not define who we are to God. For St. Paul, God sees the very face of his Son in each one of us. This will enable the not-so-poor to exercise poverty of the heart.

Many of the mortal circumstances can then be considered blessed when the reversal of values occurs. All the unfortunate conditions of the society in-deed are channels of blessedness.

God is encountered not in the human understanding of success or ideals but mostly in our helplessness. To recognize God in adversities can be a sign of tremendous faith. Jesus can then go on to explain the reward his disciples will obtain on earth for being faithful to him: false accusations, persecutions, rejection, and the unavoidable event of a death like his. But these will not be the end. These will lead to endlessness: resurrection and life eternal because no one can destroy love firmly believed and experienced in faith.

With this faith in reversal of values, a person can claim, like Paul, that God's power can be displayed in human weakness. The weak can be chosen by God to disgrace the strong. The despicable and lowly who are considered nothing can shame those who consider themselves something. When we claim nothing at all, then Christ becomes everything: righteousness, sanctification, and redemption (1 Cor 1: 26-31). According to Paul, you cannot make yourself righteous no matter how many laws you may observe because you can only be made righteous. You cannot make yourself holy because you are only being sanctified. No matter how law abiding you may be, you cannot redeem yourself but only be redeemed. You cannot earn forgiveness because it can only be given by God freely. God's forgiveness does not depend on the degree of your repentance and sorrow because it is unconditional: granted to you before, during, and after sinfulness. It can only be freely received. It is unreserved and guaranteed for the believers. What God does to you is more important than what you do for God. If everything is only a gift, then both poverty and prosperity can be blessings.

Our hearts will not rest until they rest in God

Luke 4: 14-22 (# 216)

St. Augustine struggled to understand his equal attraction both to sin and to God. Promiscuity and holiness extended identical invitations. Somewhere deep down in his heart he made a great and convincing experiential discovery: A terrible sinner and great saint are only one step away from each other. When the transference from sinful state to holiness occurs by an internal understanding, transformation is effected by the grace of God. A sinner has a right need but is addicted to a wrong fix. When God is discovered as the cause of human attractions, saintliness dawns. Having discerned the meaning of his cravings, St. Augustine proclaimed, "O God, our hearts have been created for Thee, and they will not rest until they rest in Thee."

Coming to his own native town of Nazareth, where he was accustomed to going to the synagogue, Jesus stood up to read the scriptures. When the scroll of the prophet Isaiah was handed to him, he unrolled it and found the passage where it was written: "The spirit of the Lord is upon me." Jesus will go on to read how he had been chosen to proclaim the good news to the poor and abandoned, liberation to the enslaved, healing to the blind, freedom to the oppressed, and that the year of the Lord is at hand. To the crowd who listened to him attentively he stated, "This scripture passage is fulfilled in your hearing."

Although he read the same message of Isaiah prophesied many centuries before to the captives in Babylon, Jesus attaches an entirely different meaning of spiritual liberation from sin. Jesus did not fight the Romans, nor did he heal all the blind or free the oppressed. In his miracles, Jesus would often point out that he was freeing people from the power of Satan. He did many signs and performed miracles to let his contemporaries know that the root cause of all human desires was an intrinsic draw toward God. He invited the audience to recognize that if the true desire was for God, then they had to acknowledge the coming of his Son among them to fulfill that need. This is why he proclaimed himself to be food from heaven and life-giving water. Food and water are our basic needs. They are real and yet they are symbolic, satisfying a hunger and thirst far deeper than the physical. The people of Israel identified their need for real shelter as their promised land here on Earth where God's Kingdom would be established. They failed to recognize how their very desires for food and shelter were meant for God.

Existential psychologists postulate an existential gap or emptiness in us. It is unbridgeable. No one causes it because it is ontological. People may blame themselves or others for it. Often, they try to fill this gap with relationship(s) or desired objects. Mystics present God as the true satisfaction of that incompleteness. Union with God alone will provide the truest oneness that eludes all human relationships. Addictive behaviors such as alcoholism can be blessings, if a person truly understands the destination of their powerful pull. Once God is held as the object of fulfillment, other cravings become less attractive because with true love earthly desires disappear and real satisfaction emerges. Love cannot be substituted for any desires. In fact, lack of love is like a bottomless pit. The more the desires remain empty and unaddressed by pure love, the more cravings emerge. That is why addictive behaviors only drain the soul and leave humans empty. Therefore there is more and more a need to reinforce or feed a greater number of addictive behaviors. The key is to address their root cause: The hole in the soul belongs only to God. If God is experienced as the true object of love, other desires recede into the background. Jesus means precisely that. Holding on to possessions will not lead to ultimate satisfaction; nor can lack of them deprive one of fulfillment. Wealth need not be a solution and poverty not a problem. Real wealth of faith can develop more from human poverty of many sorts. When everything one can hold is lost, then that "no-thing experience" will lead to God who will fill in for all that is lost and beyond what eye has not seen and ear has not heard.

Grateful means transformation within and without

Luke 17: 11-19 (# 145C/493)

In a Westchester daily The Journal News (Hughes, 2005) reported a "gift to last a lifetime" of Mike Olsen, age 40, to his younger brother Christian, age 35. As a young child, Christian was diagnosed with type I diabetes. Twelve years ago, Christian had already received a kidney and pancreas from someone who died in an automobile accident. When the doctors diagnosed the failure of the kidney two years ago, Mike "jumped right in" without even being requested by Christian to donate. Although it was scary, Mike did not hesitate to offer the gift of a lifetime. Imagine the overwhelming sense of gratitude Christian must have been feeling. True gratitude is more than being sentimental as evidenced in the gospel of Thanksgiving Day in comparing the healing of the Samaritan leper against nine other lepers.

Gratitude indicates a tremendous faith in God. As the nine other lepers proceed to the temple to show themselves to the priests, they have faith in the words of Jesus that they will be healed. But the Samaritan displays even a greater faith in Jesus after healing. As he is healed along the way with the others, he suddenly starts returning to Jesus because in him he discovers a person more significant than the temple and the priests. Unlike others who rush to fulfill formalities, he personalizes his faith in Jesus, finding in him the temple, the priests, and other rituals. Deeper faith can be religion-less. Non-Christians may possess deeper spirituality than Christians. Being faithful means our acts of worship will have to generate genuinely from the depth of our hearts, of our very being, beyond routines. On the contrary, the rituals of worship can be superficial, empty, and repetitious without being personal.

Being grateful implies recognizing God as the very significant extent of our being. Nine other lepers had faith and therefore they experienced healing. But mere physical and emotional healing is incomplete without a spiritual component. The other lepers may have gone back to their families and friends afterward to rejoice with them. But the story of the Samaritan was different. Samaritans were disliked by the Jews because they accepted only the five books of the Torah while rejecting the prophets and other writings of scripture. The Jews considered them unfaithful to God because of their different belief system. Yet this Samaritan leper experienced holistic healing by discovering Jesus as all-encompassing and fulfilling the Torah, the prophets, and the scriptures.

Without this faith in Jesus as God in a human person, he realized other support systems and, in fact, he himself would be incomplete. In fact, his trust in Jesus enables him to attain the final phase of healing. The affirmation Jesus offers the leper does not compliment him for his physical healing that resulted out of his faith. Jesus says, "Stand up and go; your faith has saved you" (Lk 17: 19). Jesus considers faith in him the real healing. Being saved through faith in him is more important than being healed physically and emotionally. Faith can enable one to experience spiritual healing even when one suffers incurable leprosy. The spiritual healing of simply trusting God can occur even in the midst of irreversible, irrecoverable physical and emotional conditions. Spiritual healing, therefore, is more required of us because it will outlast the other two, the physical and emotional, and truly save the individual.

Being grateful indicates that all of life is a free and total gift; and therefore, it has to be emptied or given away to others unreservedly, unselfishly. God has given us everything freely although we believe we earn some through our hard labor. Where do we draw the line between our efforts and gratuitous gifts? What underlies such faith is the relationship of the Three Persons of the Holy Trinity. They give and receive themselves freely and totally. There is no earning of love and therefore no withholding of love. Besides, if everything we receive is a gift, then we should accept our missed opportunities, mistakes, weaknesses, and imperfections as gifts just as Paul did. Because our gifts are gratuitous, they have to be emptied completely for the sake of one another. That means there is no room for selfishness, greed, manipulation of others, partial commitments, and divided loyalties. Gratitude means more than simply being sentimental.

Last judgment has already begun

Matthew 25: 31-46 (# 161A)

In the 12th century, Saint Elizabeth of Hungary, the daughter of King Andrew of Hungary, was given in marriage to Ludwig of Thuringia as a young girl, and she bore him three children. Strikingly, even as a queen, she was drawn to poverty and devoted to mental prayer. She built a hospice near one of her castles. Every morning and evening she visited the sick who suffered from the foulest diseases, feeding them, carrying them in her arms, and cleaning their pallets. After the death of her beloved husband, she entered the third order of St. Francis and renounced herself of her own will. Whatever property she inherited she bequeathed to the poor, keeping only one worn- out dress in which she wanted to be buried. In St. Elizabeth, internal transformation remarkably blended with external works of charity. Her transformation was as much indicative of deep faith as it was of her good works of mercy. Her interior transformation and exterior activities remained at one and the same level.

Matthew frames the public ministry of Jesus with messages of blessedness. Jesus calls "blessed" those who are poor in spirit, or mourn, know hunger and thirst, and the merciful (5: 3- 10). Here he calls "blessed by my Father" those who have reached out to the poor, the grieving, the hungry and thirsty, and tells them they belong to the Kingdom (Mt 25:34). Even as this parable lends material to the imaginations of artists and poets, it has its interpretive glitches. The word used for "all generations" in general means Gentiles. Usage here includes Gentiles, Jews, and Christians, and it implies a collective responsibility of nations as well as individuals. It is erroneous to read the context as referring either to Gentiles and Jews versus Christians, or even to believers versus nonbelievers. There is the danger of distinguishing between humanitarian acts of mercy and those that are done in Jesus' name. All are called and the good are separated from the evil. Least of my brothers may imply more to Christian missionaries who bore the brunt of evangelization than those who are poor, hungry, ill, or naked. Missionaries share similar states.

Those who indulged in acts of mercy appear to be rewarded for their good works. Good deeds seem to be ways of gaining the Kingdom. "Faith versus good works" has been a debatable issue with regard to their priority as aids to entry into God's Kingdom. We are reminded of Paul's struggle with law versus faith. Psychologically, it boils down to external observations versus their internalization. Anything performed without a corresponding interiorization is hypocritical. To the degree one is transformed by faith, one can/should involve oneself in external charity. However, it is possible to be humanitarian without faith in Christ. Faith in Jesus will demand more and offer more hope than mere humanitarianism. Likewise, whatever charity is carried on externally should enable one to develop a deeper faith in God.

When this mutuality exists, then there will be no additions or distinctions between one's state of being and saying, doing, or performing. It is the "uncalculated, unintended giving" that surprises the sheep grouped on the right side during the last judgment. Because response of the charitable was such a natural, spontaneous, unpretentious, and instinctive act of a loving heart, their generous acts were never even recorded in their memory. Since God's Kingdom is an unearned, undeserved, and gratuitous gift given to both the good and the bad, it cannot be earned through banking acts of mercy and compassion. In fact, the Kingdom has already been given in the person of Jesus. Therefore, it is more a matter of letting that Kingdom transform one now than one acquiring it at the end through accumulation of acts of mercy (Barclay, 2001).

Although both deeper faith as well as acts of mercy is simultaneously needed, faith should precede acts of generosity to be the sheep. In fact, even the last judgment has already been initiated and we have the choice of judging ourselves by choosing which side we want to be on. We will only be exposed to its final stage at the end. Final judgment has become our here-and-now responsibility and option.

What about the poor, the hungry, the ill, the naked, and the imprisoned who may not be able to afford good works? They are tested in their faith. Their situations may prevent them from seeing themselves as blessed as they suffer indignity. The reason Jesus speaks these words before he begins his passion is to imply that he himself will share their plight, but will not distrust himself to be the(ir) king. It is this message that will challenge the disciples to see him as their king even as he suffers ignominy.

Forgive in order to be forgiven

Matthew 18: 21-35 (# 131A)

How do you see yourself moments after death? The following is someone's fantasy: "Right after my death I will be shut into a dark room with no windows and doors. My one other companion will be the person I least loved and was unable to forgive. Outside the room is eternal glory. The only way to be drawn into that light is to be together with this person until I get comfortable and feel forgiveness." The hatred I feel today will continue to eternity. In the National Highway Traffic Safety Administration's statistics on automobile accidents a large percentage is attributed to aggressive driving or road rage. The media is inundated with hate crimes among ethnic groups in Northern Ireland, the Middle East, and countries in Europe, Africa, the Americas, and Asia. There appears to be an intrinsic relationship between unwillingness to forgive and anger as its root cause.

In the gospel, the very question of Peter is wrong for two reasons: First, it does not seem to be concerned with the unrepentant frequent offender; second, its expectation of a boundary for the extent of forgiveness is in direct opposition to God's endless mercy. In explaining the position of an unforgiving servant, Jesus puts him on par with the frequent offender, making him no better than the offender. First of all, the parable portrays the limitless forgiveness of the king when the debtor is unable to repay the loan. It is impossible to earn or deserve forgiveness for sins against God no matter the level of repentance. It is a gratuitous gift; therefore, forgiveness and love of God are two sides of the same coin.

To love is to forgive and to forgive is to love. Even without the requirement of repentance, pardon is ever granted before, during, or after the offense. Therefore, forgiveness has to be experienced more in faith than in repentance itself. Humans are used to earning, deserving forgiveness. That is why even the unrepentant offender is simply written off. It may not belong to you only if you do not believe and act as if you have already been forgiven.

The servant whose burdensome debt was freely forgiven is very harsh with a fellow servant who owed him only a small amount of money. Why he was unable to forgive him has not been explained. Was he highly insensitive, harsh, crude, and angry with him? We don't know. All that we know is that he remained unrepentant and unforgiving to the point of throwing the debtor into prison. Because he withholds his forgiveness, he shuts out God's freely offered forgiveness. Whatever he does to the miserable debtor he is actually inflicting upon himself right now. He misses the guaranteed way of obtaining God's mercy because of his own lack of forgiveness for the debtor. He fails to build a heavenly kingdom here on Earth. What an extraordinary gift it would be from God to accept pardon and mercy and then show the same to others. He misses this golden opportunity.

Receiving this gift from God is made all the more possible because we start entering into the heavenly kingdom here on Earth. It is made available as a choice, an option. Our heavenly kingdom will not be a surprise because it has already been given to us as an option in our relationship with Jesus and with one another. It further draws us to understand that the judgment of God is also an option available to us. Our unwillingness to forgive is justified through anger which derives from our judgmental attitude. Since we constantly judge ourselves, justifying our decisions, God allows us to continue until we see clearly at the moment of death what we have done to ourselves. Therefore, Jesus said, "Stop judging that you may not be judged" (Mt 7:1). Whatever we bind on earth will be bound in heaven. The only way to release anger and a judgmental mindset is to forgive. Forgiving and asking for forgiveness are both healing because forgiveness itself is a reflection of love. True love lies beyond our anger. Anger can make one violent, depressive, suicidal, and unforgiving. Unwillingness to forgive others is unwillingness to repent for our own sins.

The Kingdom of God is more about generosity than justice

Matthew 20: 1-16 (# 134A)

In the world of commerce, the logic Jesus applies to the parable does not seem to be just. Listening to the proclamation of the gospel somehow hints to us that there is something we understand but also something we don't. All the same, as Jesus' words point out, justice is not violated, our sense of injustice remains. The parable follows the rich young man's question, "Teacher, what good must I do to gain eternal life?" (Mt 19: 16) and Peter's inquiry, "We have given up everything and followed you. What will there be for us?" (Mt 19: 27) and Jesus' response, "But many who are first will be last, and the last will be first" (Mt 19: 30). The young man who thought he had earned riches from God through his faithful observance of the Law was troubled when Jesus asked him to go and sell all he had and give it to the poor in order to have riches in heaven, because it conflicted with his idea of gaining rewards through good behaviors. Through Peter, the disciples are told that their dispossessing material things will reward them a hundred times over.

Both, the rich man and Peter, had only a partial idea of the Kingdom as a reward. Jesus does not deny that the Kingdom is a reward. But he continues to say that it is more than simply remuneration. It is an act of generosity on the part of God. This parable will portray a dimension of his Kingdom that was unimaginable to his contemporaries as well as to us. The landowner goes out into the streets looking for laborers. The workers are unable to find jobs on their own until they find the landlord. The landowner freely invites them to work, not at the request of the laborers. The manner of the landowner to go out into the streets many different times of the day shows that the workers are invited without examination of their capabilities, regardless of their talents. Even the end of the day did not stop the landowner from withholding an invitation to laborers. The foreman is instructed to start paying from the last to the first which is unusual. Those that came last receive first a day's wage which is more than being fair. The ones who came first presume that their earnings should exceed that of those who started working very late because they had worked longer. Their complaint does not constitute an injustice because they were contracted for a day's wage and they were paid accordingly.

They gripe about the generosity of the landowner and feel that their hard labor has not been fully acknowledged by him. Justice was served however, because the landowner treated all the laborers equally, with no regard for the amount of work each actually produced.

God's Kingdom must be a reward for those who faithfully observe all that is required here on Earth. While the words of Jesus reveal that there will be such a reward, they also manifest an idea that it will be more than a reward. It will be simply a gift, bestowed upon even those who did not seem to deserve it here on Earth. The Kingdom is as much a gratuity as it is a reward. No one deserves it, because it is being offered to the undeserving as well. The Pharisees, who observed everything prescribed by the law, failed to acknowledge the extravagant generosity expressed in and through Jesus. The Kingdom is more about the person of Jesus than about any blessing, because Jesus is the Kingdom.

Relationship with him is not earned but freely offered. Everyone is accepted. Jesus had no problem having parties with tax collectors, prostitutes, the sick, the unchurched, and the underprivileged, all of whom were told that they did not earn God's blessings. Merely possessing material blessings and physical well-being need not be signs of saintliness, but they could possibly be a sign of sinfulness. Being disregarded by the world due to a lack of blessings and even being addicted to sins cannot deprive one of the Kingdom because of the person of Jesus. Therefore, sin is a choice resulting from refusal to receive forgiveness freely offered in the person of Jesus. It is the acknowledgment of God's love that will enable one to see that love is more about generosity which is boundless than about justice which is limited. While justice has to do with reward, generosity invites one to accept the kingdom freely in the person of Jesus.

God loves us not out of justice but mercy and generosity

Matthew 21: 28-32 (# 137A)

In Holy Rosary Church in Port Chester, New York, the deacon in charge of the food pantry began to notice a steady rise in the number of needy people in the past few years. In this wealthy part of the country, there seemed an increase in poverty that had gone unnoticed. In a report to the Westchester daily The Journal News, the deacon attributed such an increase to "a lack of morality" of the people. How he explained that was surprising. "Too many people are greedy today. What the greedy do not recognize is that the desire to possess more than required deprives others of their sustenance." While in general lack of morality is characterized as sexual sin, the deacon suggests another manifestation of immorality from his deeper understanding of the concept and how this immorality injures others without the person's awareness. A moral behavior has to be examined more than within its context in order to assess its impact.

Jesus triumphantly entered Jerusalem. After being welcomed by hosannas, he assumes his responsibilities as the royal king in the temple, first by cleansing it boldly and then by curing people. His tone of authority shocks the Pharisees and the scribes who then question him about the basis for his authority. Instead of answering, Jesus questions them about the source of John the Baptist's authority. Although they know the answer, they respond by saying they do not. Jesus then relates this simple parable which will force them to answer and judge themselves. When the father asks one of his sons to go to work in the vineyard he says "no" but then he regrets his decision and complies with his father's request. The other son immediately says "yes," but then disregards his promise and does not abide by it. The Pharisees and Scribes easily answer his question, but the explanation that Jesus offered must have shocked them.

The son who says "no" to the father and then later ends up doing the opposite in the story is then compared to the tax collectors and prostitutes who are last in society's estimation but are the first to enter the Kingdom of God. Jesus tells the religious leaders that they are already entering God's Kingdom, because of their choice of God in Jesus. They are the ones who initially rebel against the law as many of us who search for God in the wrong places. It was greed that motivated the tax collector to look for love in falsely embracing money as the object of love despite opposition and disapproval from his fellow Jews. He knows he is wrong and does not deserve to go to the temple because of his view of himself as a terrible sinner. Similarly the prostitute, who centers her experience of love on sensual pleasures and easy money, knows that she is guilty and shameful.

Their encounters with Jesus were experienced as being exceptional because Jesus' acceptance of them as worthy human beings shocks them. Jesus loves the sinners but not their sins. He is able to distinguish sinners from sinfulness. He loves them for what they are and not for what they do. What they encounter is an extraordinary exposure to the epitome of love. Their craving for addictive behaviors such as greed and lust is actually a longing for a most satisfying love in the person of Jesus. When love comes into their lives, the objects of their material cravings lose their attraction.

The other son follows the order of his father and appears to please him when he says "yes," but does not in fact internalize his love for the father. His impersonalized familial dedication does not move beyond the letter of the law. He believes that he will get away by pretending to obey the father. The Pharisees and Scribes believed whatever is ritually observed would entitle them to the Kingdom. Jesus tells them they cannot earn the Kingdom through right behaviors because God's love for humans is not between two equals. God's love is not in response to our morality but out of mercy and generosity. The undeserved are loved because God is purely merciful and generous, a revelation far beyond the minds of the religious leaders because such love is extravagant and scandalous to their mundane minds.

Believers can reject God through resistances

Matthew 21: 33-43 (# 140A)

Having entered the city, Jesus has a series of confrontations with the chief priest and the elders of the people. Time is running out and their resistance to him becomes greater. They start looking for an opportunity to kill him but are afraid of the people. They begin to question him. Instead of answering their questions, Jesus will raise questions to which they refuse to respond. But finally, through parables Jesus will allow them to judge themselves. Jesus becomes more and more candid about the way they will later treat him. Through the parables, he confirms the predictions of his own passion and death.

After the response to the question regarding the two sons, Jesus compares the son who refuses to go into the vineyard to work, but later does, to the tax collectors and prostitutes, and the religious leaders to the other son who says he will go to work but does not. In this parable, Jesus recalls the imagery of a vineyard (Is 5: 1-7) and a friend's song concerning his vineyard. Even though the friend labors hard and plants choice vines, they yield only wild grapes. The owner then chooses to ruin the vineyard by removing the hedge and letting it be trampled.

Jesus alludes not only to the work of the landowner in creating the vineyard but also to the servants who follow later to warn the tenants of their refusal to return the produce. They beat, stone, and kill the servants who are the prophets of the Old and New Testament. Almost naively the landowner sends his only son who he thinks will be respected by the tenants. His fate becomes nothing more than that of the servants who preceded him. Jesus describes dramatically how they will turn on him also and crucify him outside the city. As expected, the religious leaders answer him by letting him know that the landowner will punish the wretched people with death.

In recalling Jesus' words, Matthew relates them to his contemporaries, the Jewish leaders who continued to oppose him even after the death and resurrection of Christ. He adds references to the exaltation of the risen Savior by quoting Psalm 118: 22-23. God offsets human tragedy with the resurrection of his Son, disregarding human follies. It is ironic that the leaders in the establishment reject God in the person of Jesus even though they claim to worship him. Devout Christians can also reject God through resistances. Resistance for us may be in the form of expressed or subtle denials. As believers, we can choose to act as unbelievers when we become frozen in fear, guilt, shame, blame, depression, anxiety, anger, sorrow, unwillingness to admit or let go of losses, addictions, addictive behaviors, and most notably, arrogance. When we become stuck in these attitudes, we build resistances as did the religious leaders of Jesus' time. We are called to believe and trust in God not in the absence or removal of debilitating turmoil, but precisely in their midst as we experience them.

The good news has to be believed in the midst of bad news, not in its absence. Jesus preached the good news that requires extraordinary open-mindedness. The religious leaders were so set in their ways that they only saw limited points of view because they seemed to understand God logically with a linear-thinking mind. Observation of laws was a guarantee that they were working their way to heaven. But what they failed to realize was the demand of God to internalize their external observations, to personalize their relationship as opposed to ritualizing it. Therefore, sinners such as the Gentiles will embrace the Kingdom not through right observation of laws but faith in God's Son, Jesus. To relate to Jesus, all our expectations about God will have to be abandoned and God must simply be embraced in all of life's happenings, good and bad. Only those who do not hold on to any resistance will let God in.

Acting with mercy is more important than doing it right

Luke 10: 25-37 (# 461)

The seventy-two disciples return to Jesus after their first missionary adventure. Excitedly they report how they saw impossible things happening by merely using his name. Jesus joins them in their elation and exults how the powers of evil were destroyed through the faith exercised by unlettered men. Jesus thanks the Father for having hidden these things from the wise and the learned and for revealing them to the mere childlike disciples. The scene undergoes a dramatic shift when a scholar of the law asks Jesus what is required of him to "inherit (gain) eternal life." The questioner stands in stark contrast to the simple disciples whose names have already been written in heaven and, in fact, had already entered heaven through their faith in him.

Questioned by Jesus about how he reads the law, the scholar quotes Scripture concerning the love of God and neighbor. Jesus affirms his interpretation. He approves of the scholar's answer but makes it known that mere observation of the law is the minimum required. The scholar needs a further explanation of how to apply the love of God to the love of neighbor. Maybe he intends to show he was correct in his understanding. Jesus relates the story of the man who fell into the hands of robbers and tells how he was saved by a Samaritan in order to help the questioner expand his understanding of the law.

As the story unfolds, the scholar of the law is able to understand the situation experienced by the priest and the Levite, who upon seeing the victim, walk away from him for fear of being defiled and thus become unable to enter the temple. They do what was required according to the laws prescribed. From a legal perspective they do everything rightly and correctly. They love to live the law as they believed it was a demonstration of their faithfulness to God. They act out of justice. They are after all used to living righteously and thus feel entitled to God's Kingdom.

When the Samaritan comes on the scene, he does something that is just the opposite. He is not supposed to touch a Jew. Jews considered the Samaritans outcasts because they freely chose to break away from the belief system of the Jews. Contact with a Samaritan would render a Jew defiled. Moreover, he ran the risk of reprisals from fellow Jews. Yet, the Samaritan is prepared to risk his life rather than leave a man to die on the road. He applies oil and wine to the man's wounds and sets him on his animal to carry him to an inn. He stays with the wounded man for the day and, before leaving the next day, he pays two silver coins to the innkeeper and promises to pay more if needed. He does not want the injured man to be burdened or threatened again with any retaliation. He assumes full responsibility. Even though it was not expected of him to help the Jew, the Samaritan acts out of mercy and generosity. He chooses to love an undeserving, injured man. The Samaritan has every reason to curse him and feel as though he deserved the hatred shown to him by the Jews. It was fair and just that the Jew deserved such a plight for dissociating himself from the Samaritans. Yet, he preferred to act out of mercy and generosity and not out of justice, which would have been "an eye for an eye and a tooth for a tooth."

The scholar of the law had so much justifiable hatred for the Samaritans that he could not bring himself to call the man who helped the victim a Samaritan. Instead he calls him "the one who treated him with mercy." Human love is based on justice by acting rightly and correctly. With divine love, none of us deserves to be loved by God; we only need God's mercy and forgiveness. God loves us out of mercy and generosity. We are then called to love the undeserving because our love from God is unearned. God's love within the Three Persons of the Trinity is unearned, free, and unconditional.

Believers can be paying lip service to God

Matthew 22: 1-10 (# 143A)

Following the aftermath of the devastating hurricanes Katrina and Rita in 2005, moving stories of unsung heroes were reported in the media. After being exposed suddenly to violent winds and flooding that tragically destroyed their own homes and property, some individuals rushed from home to home in motorboats trying to save thousands of lives. A young woman from a faraway place took a leave of absence from her well-paying banking career and rushed to help the victims in shelters. Through her own experiences in the bank she cut through the red tape that had frustrated and delayed people's entitlements to emergency measures. Two air marshals were sent down to search the thousands of homes of those who had called 911 and were not reached. They wanted to determine if people in their flooded homes moved to safety or perished (The Journal News). To the degree one is drawn into the tragedy, one will respond to it.

Although the Pharisees and the elders of the people of Israel claimed to be faithful in their worship of Yahweh, they, in fact, remained unbelievers. Their fanatical observation of external obligations did not entitle them to the Kingdom but in fact obstructed them from moving forward. Their worship of God was merely mechanical rather than personal. They claimed to justify themselves through righteousness contrary to being justified only by God, as Paul understood. The Kingdom is compared to the wedding feast the king offered for his son. Luke paints a picture of it as a mere meal (14: 15-24). The image is an eschatological banquet God promised at the end of times (Is 25: 6). The Pharisees fail to recognize the invitation as merely gratuitous but perceive it as exclusive because of their Jewish origin and faithful observations of the laws. Initially, the invitation was extended to the specially chosen guests, the people of Israel and its religious leaders. The prophets of the Old and New Testament up to John the Baptist were not listened to but rather tortured and even put to death. In their ritualism, they were more engrossed with their mundane business and refused to establish a personal relationship with God.

The post-resurrection writing of Matthew reflects the same resistance Jesus faced from his contemporaries. Jewish missionaries were opposed by fellow Jews. Their resistance leads to the wrath of the king in the destruction of the temple of Jerusalem in 70 A.D. Now the outcasts are invited because of their continued refusal to believe in Jesus Christ. The good and the evil ones among the Gentiles, together with those Jewish believers, now form a new group of invitees: the Church. The story then takes a new twist as the king visits his honored guests.

One of them is found with improper dress and is handpicked to be thrown into the darkness "where there will be wailing and grinding of teeth" (Mt 22:13). Even though saints and sinners are being called only a few will be chosen. There is no entitlement earned, but rather one is expected to be merely receptive to the unearned gift. The reception is measured against one's readiness. The selection is through the process of judgment whereby the individual is helped to see clearly whether or not earthly worship had really transformed the person into a new creation in Christ. Paul identifies the wedding garment: "Put on then...heartfelt compassion, kindness, humility, gentleness, and patience....And over all these virtues put on love" (Col 3:12-14). What Matthew is saying is that it is one thing to be a member of the Church but it is quite another to be saved. Members can exercise mechanical worship rather than have faith that leads to total transformation. This faith can lead a believer to reflect the mind of Paul, "I know indeed how to live in humble circumstances; I know also how to live with abundance" (Phil 4:12). Without transformation, worship will simply be lip service.

Earthly matters are not so significant as heavenly ones

Matthew 22: 15-21 (# 146A)

The Roman General (later emperor) Titus ordered the temple of Jerusalem to be razed in 70 A.D. Before the troops destroyed the veil that covered the Holy of Holies of the temple, he personally desired to investigate what was behind it. It was so sacred that even the High Priest was allowed to enter it only once a year. Trampling over the bodies of the Jewish freedom fighters and priests, he pulled down the veil and with roaring laughter commented, "I have resolved the riddle of the Jews. There is nothing behind." It is ironic that what was everything to the Jews was found to be nothing to a Gentile. Domitian Caesar was puzzled about how a crucified Jewish criminal known as Christ could detract from the emperor's cult. When he was ordered to bring before Caesar the treasures of the Church, John the apostle took along a widow, a beggar, and an orphan and claimed them to be treasures. Laughing uncontrollably, Ceasar exiled John to the island of Patmos and persecuted the Christians.

After the Pharisees and the elders were made to answer their own questions, they retreated to plot Jesus' murder. Their disciples along with Herodians were sent to "entrap" Jesus. The Pharisees did not like dealing with Roman coins because it was a stark reminder of their slavery. Besides, the coins contained the image of the emperor with the words, "Tiberius Caesar, son of the divine Augustus, high priest." Strictly forbidden to use any image of God, they were subjected to handle it for a human being they hated. While the Pharisees hated the census tax, the Herodians supported it. Enemies divided by their beliefs now joined to entrap a common enemy. When Jesus asked for a coin they readily produced one, a sign of contradiction -- while hating the law they obeyed the earthly king. Jesus' words, "Repay to Caesar what belongs to Caesar and to God what belongs to God," seem to satisfy both parties. Jesus did not oppose payment of taxes and so subsequently be identified as a revolutionary as the Pharisees had expected. He did not disappoint the Herodians. Nor did he offend the devout and observant Jews who did not see the justification of the taxes to the Roman government that enslaved them.

On a deeper level, the answer of Jesus leads us to a far different insight. If everything belongs to God, whatever Caesar owned also was

God's. Owe to God everything, and owe to Caesar nothing because he had nothing. Even though the religious leaders did not claim to owe any allegiance to the emperor they were more concerned with worldly matters than those of God.

While they thought of their Roman slavery as a problem to be resolved by God, Jesus identified slavery to sin as the problem separating humans from God. The Pharisees attempted to go to heaven by righteousness, knowing and performing it right. Jesus told them they could not do it right unless it was made right by God. Paul would introduce the concept of justification precisely in opposition to this unequivocal claim. Therefore, they persisted in their belief even up to the crucifixion of Jesus which was a righteous thing according to the Pharisees. That one terrible "wrong" was indeed made "right" by God, ironically making all humans, including the Jews, truly "righteous" before God. Only God can make us righteous.

We promise to place all our faith and trust in God, but we make every effort to defend, protect, acquire, succeed, and win. We compromise the gratuitous gifts from God with our own efforts. We forget the fine line between our efforts and the free, unearned, unmerited gifts of God. Rather than saying, "God provided for me and I received from God," often we justify our modes of acquiring, succeeding, deserving, and earning through our own merits. We tend to put human achievement over what is freely given as a gift from God, everything. Earthly matters seem to be more of a concern to us than recognizing freely flowing gifts from heaven.

Law means love

Matthew 22: 34-40 (# 149A)

In the aftermath of hurricanes Katrina and Rita that devastated New Orleans, CNN reported a paramedic nurse's selfless services. The nurse volunteered to travel in a huge boat along with other officials who set out to check on the sick and the elderly who rode out the storms. The nurse cared for the survivors and encouraged them to continue monitoring themselves. When the brave souls met her they were moved to tears at how caring she was without knowing her own story. The nurse's own home was completely ravaged by the flood waters, and she was staying in temporary housing that she generously shared with her children and grandchildren. Even though her home and entire family were in disarray, she wasted no time looking for the helpless. When questioned by the interviewer she said that she always enjoyed her duty because she did things from her heart. She added that the job kept her from being overly concerned about her own tragedy, so she was prepared to lend herself wholeheartedly to the demands of other disrupted people.

Instead of merely fulfilling her role as a dutiful person, the nurse enjoyed it as a dedication and devotion. She transcended the law to a sphere of love and commitment. When a person starts engaging himself/herself from the minimum to the maximum, he/she moves to the spiritual dimension of love. Questioned by a Pharisee, a scholar of the law, about the greatest commandment of the law, Jesus responds with two kinds of love (Mt 22: 37-39). In Mark the interaction between the scribes and Jesus is casual, while in Matthew it occurs in a controversy (Mk 12: 28-34). In Mark there is an order or a hierarchy in the two kinds of love, love of God (Deut 6: 4-5) and of neighbor (Lev 19:18) as quoted by Jesus. Unlike Mark's account, Matthew's Jesus links the second to the first command with the phrase "like it" (Mt 22: 39), which though a big difference, still maintains Mark's order. Love of God is first and love of neighbor is second, but it is equal to the first. They are both the first and greatest commandments.

Love of God has to be exercised wholeheartedly, discarding half-hearted, superficial, and divided loyalties. In the name of love of God, a few obligations may be fulfilled routinely without interiorization, as the Pharisees did. They faithfully adhered to the 248 positive commandments and the 365 prohibitions that formed the legal corpus. Among them Jesus picked out two important commandments that insist on love of God and neighbor. Jesus implies love has to take precedence over law. The very idea of law appears to go against love because it curtails our liberty. Laws by their nature threaten us with punishment in the case of nonobservance. Compliance with the law can result from fear of consequences, as others look for ways to circumvent laws. When laws are taken to heart, the response will be doubled or tripled depending on the level of love with which one carries them out. Law is just the start, but love is endless. When transcendence occurs, the person crosses the boundary and is liberated from the law which is what Jesus is inviting the religious leaders to do. But they remained self-righteous and never did anything more than what was required. Their love of God was equated with mere fulfillment of external obligations.

The Pharisees saw themselves earning righteousness through obedience. But Jesus sees them as arrogant, legalistic, and judgmental. Their observance blinded them to being transformed into the ideal Son of God that Jesus was. The information received from the law did not lead to the transformation God expected, because their relationship with God was impersonal just as their external observance was mechanical. Unless one loves the laws and acts motivated by love, abiding by the law will only be a lip service. Repetitious fulfillment of obligations may have no effect on the individual who practices them unless the person understands law means love.

What we say and do versus who we are

Matthew 23: 1-14 (# 152A)

Having encountered God in a mystical relationship, great mystics speak a language of exceptional love. Their words are intriguing. Our hearts seem to be drawn to them more than our reason. St. Francis of Assisi, a stigmatic and a nature mystic prayed: "God, grant me the courage to change the things I can and accept the things that I cannot and the wisdom to know the difference." We also sing the song of his prayer: "Lord, make me an instrument of your peace. Where there is hatred, let me bring love. Where there is injury your pardon, Lord. And where there is doubt, true faith in you." He prayed not so much to be understood as to understand. St. Francis, who pairs paradoxes so masterfully, said to his fellow brothers, "Preach the gospel always. If necessary, use words." Somehow his few words seem to demonstrate how he experienced perfect love of God in his very being so that he spoke words that expressed love more than intelligence. He kept his mystical union with God secretive, but it nevertheless was transparent in his very being.

After his controversial conversation with the scribes and the Pharisees, Jesus turns to the crowds and his disciples and offers words of wisdom. The Matthean community faced expulsion from the synagogues. Pharisaic Judaism despised nonobservant Jews, known as "the children of the land," as well as Jewish Christians. Capturing the words of Jesus, Matthew has Jesus approve of the teaching authority of the religious leaders. Sternly he warns the crowd and his disciples not to follow the example of the Pharisees because they preach but do not practice their own words. The poor and the downtrodden could not bear the burden of their impositions because laws such as those related to food were not easy and sometimes impossible to follow. While the religious leaders laid onerous burdens on the people by prescribing onerous laws, they themselves had taken advantage of exceptions to their own laws.

Besides, they made a public display of their performances. They wanted to be seen as law-abiding. Enlarging phylacteries, small containers that held scripture passages, they tied them around their forehead and forearms. Lengthening of tassels indicated their law observance. They indulged in ostentation of these behaviors. They loved places of honor at banquets and primary seats in synagogues and greetings in market places. Their external elaborations did not correspond to the inner conversion of their heart and mind. Jesus then goes on to tell his disciples and the crowd not to call anyone "Rabbi" (my great one), teacher, father, or master. What we see is how a great one or teacher may not live up to his/her own words. The earthly masters may only exploit the servants without proper compensation for labor. Even our parents can fall short of their roles and disappoint us. Jesus promises to fill in for every one of these. Jesus can genuinely say these words because he means what he says. Humans can say "yes" and mean "no" and vice versa.

In opposition to their attitude, Jesus proposes his model of spirituality by inviting the audience not to seek public approval but to humbly serve one another unnoticed. Humble and hidden holiness is a mark of greatness in God's ways. What is hidden then can be very self-evident provided it transforms one deep down in one's very being. Conversely, contradictions between who you are and who you say you are will also be self-evident. Whatever one says in words and does in performances can stand apart from one's very being that can go unaffected by these. There can be an unknowing distance between our saying and doing versus our very being. People like St. Paul can say honestly that "we were determined to share with you not only the gospel of God, but our very selves as well" (1 Thess 2: 8). Disregarding his right to a stipend for his work as an apostle, he chose to preach the gospel for free. To the degree he had been transformed by God's word in his very life, he was able to reveal God not merely in his words and actions but in his very being. The call then is to bridge the gap between our saying/doing and our being.

It is more about being rather than about earning

Matthew 25: 1-13 (# 155A)

Father Jerome Schaad, a religious priest of the Sacred Heart of Jesus, served his provincial headquarters in Milwaukee, Wisconsin, as the provincial treasurer. Illustrious and energetic as he was, he took ill suddenly and died of a rare form of cancer. During the eulogy, the provincial said how he had asked the men of his community to write down scripture readings for their funeral liturgy. After Fr. Schaad's death when his particular notation was sought the words that appeared on his sheet were: "Surprise me." Knowing Fr. Schaad as a friend, I can vouch for his ever readiness with his work. Although one may wonder if he did not think it was too early to be asked for funeral directions, I presume he was ever ready to meet his Creator. The gospel today asks us to begin preparation for our end right now.

Pointing to the temple buildings, Jesus says to his disciples "there will not be left here a stone upon another stone that will not be thrown down" (Mt 24: 2). The disciples approach him in private and say, "Tell us, when will this happen, and what sign will there be of your coming, and of the end of the age?" (Mt 24: 3). Jesus then begins to make predictions about future persecutions and great tribulations. After the tribulations, the powers of heaven will be shaken, and signs will appear in heaven before the Son of Man "coming upon the clouds of heaven with power and great glory" (Mt 24: 30). The question of how to be prepared will then be explained by Jesus in the following sections (Mt 24: 32-50). The parable of Ten Virgins has to be examined in the context of the Matthean Jewish Christian community that was expelled from the synagogues by the mainstream Jewish leadership. Even after the death and resurrection of Jesus, first century Judaism opposed any allegiance to Jesus. The story demonstrates what was still missing with the Jews although they were expecting the Messiah for the first time.

As the parable unfolds, one finds it hard to imagine that Jesus would be so hard as to deny knowing people who claim to have known him. It is possible to imagine Jesus encouraging even those who know him only slightly. Likewise, it is equally difficult to imagine Jesus tolerating the wise virgins being unkind at the time of the coming of the groom and refusing to share the oil for the lamps. This parable may be erroneously interpreted as an allegory by comparing the bridegroom to Jesus and the unwise virgins to those that were unprepared. If interpreted as a parable, it insists on the lesson of being prepared for the coming of the Son of Man. It portrays eschatological events, such as the end of times, the returning of Jesus, the resurrection of all believers, heaven and hell, and so on. While the Jewish Christian community may be compared to the wise virgins, the unwise may be compared to Jewish leadership that missed the essence of Jesus' message that was required for deep transformation. When applied to the Christian community itself one can see how believers themselves can experience a sense of unbelief at the coming of Jesus because of a lukewarm relationship. Knowing and committing halfheartedly will lead to unknowing and rejection in the end.

In traditional exegesis, the oil and the lights are represented as good works of charity, the mission activity. But even such performances can be extraneous without the interior transformation. Knowing Jesus fully and being transformed by his words and deeds cannot be borrowed from any institution. Nor can the transformation be brought about by external performances. It is deeply personal, and acts of charity and generosity should flow from it. They should ideally be coexisting and also be mutually inclusive. Trusting God in the midst of devastating situations of abandonment, loneliness, betrayal, poverty, hunger, injustices, and helplessness is a mark of deep transformation. Trust cannot be earned through good works but should enable one to experience the embrace of God in our very being. Who we are is more important than what we do. The end is experienced in the now. Transformation cannot happen overnight. Vigilance to encounter Him at the end begins right now, not at the end. It takes great faith to believe that the end has already begun as has the Kingdom of God.

Watchful means embrace uncertainties

Mark 13: 33-37 (# 2B)

In November 2005 at New York's Kennedy International Airport, there was a poignant reunion of two women after half a century of separation before reporters, camera crews, and photographers. Joanna Zalucka, 82, of Poland arrived to visit Ruth Grener, 72, of Brooklyn. Joanna's family offered shelter to Ruth, then 8 years old, when she was smuggled out of the ghetto by her father during the Nazi killing spree in Poland. It was a horrible nightmare for a little girl to listen to the ransacking of Jewish homes. She had to hide under Joanna's bed or inside a trunk, a frequent exercise that immobilized her. Later Ruth and her family managed to move to Brooklyn, and she was blessed to be reunited with her savior. Thanks to the Jewish Foundation for the Righteous (The Journal News). Unless we experience a horrible situation of this sort, it would be hard to imagine so dramatic an end of one's life. The words of Jesus are relevant to such tragedies (Mk 13: 33-37).

The disciples commented on how the temple buildings glittered in grandeur. Jesus predicted how not a stone will be left upon another (Mk 13: 2). When Peter, James, John, and Andrew asked what sign there would be before such destruction, Jesus referred to false prophets who would claim to be him and how nation will rise against nation and kingdom against kingdom; and many other earthly catastrophes like earthquakes and famines would occur (13: 6-8). Adding to the misery, persecution would require believers to give witness to Jesus, even as they were arraigned before kings and governors (13: 9). The faithful would be hated by all because of his name (13: 13). But after tribulation, the universal powers would be shaken before the Son of Man would appear in the clouds (13: 26). Set in the context of Jewish history the day of the Lord meant the long awaited intervention of God, when all enemies of Israel would be defeated, and a new world and new age would then fully belong to the chosen people forever.

Jesus' parable includes several allegorical details. Jesus is the Lord of the house, and he refers to his upcoming absence through his passion and death as his traveling abroad. Because he is to be gone he delegates the management of the house to his servants and gatekeepers. "Waiting time" denotes the delay of the Parousia. Servants are simply asked to act for him. Mark points out how authority is exercised in humble service. Earlier words such as "this generation will not pass away until all these things have taken place" (13: 30) appear to indicate that the Parousia will occur even before the contemporaries of Jesus die. But then no one, except the Father, not even the Son, knows the hour (13: 32). Reflecting on the delay in coming, Mark's community appears to focus on what has to be done in the interim rather than the end.

As predicted by Jesus, the temple has already been destroyed and persecution has become rampant, but there is no return of the Son of Man. Suddenly, the words of caution from Jesus reveal implied meanings. Depicted against the background of the captivity of Israel, Jesus presents the eschatological prophecies on the heels of his passion and death. His cross will be a scandal to the disciples and believers who will wonder about his position as the Son of God as he undergoes the pains and sorrows of life and death. Unanswered questions and continued doubts will rock his followers. Against this background of uncertainties, vigilance means continued trust and faith in God. Unbearable realities may indicate the absence and loss or lack of control by the Master. How can these tragedies happen and still God does not intervene? They may be tempted to control the situations and act inappropriately for the landlord by resorting to fiery defense or ruthless violence. Instead of retaliation they are simply asked to trust beyond death. Our personal calamities are tantamount to persecution and martyrdom. Just as God was actively present in the seemly passive sufferings of Jesus, so we are called upon to trust the presence of God even as we experience Godless situations. Vigilance means continued trust and persistence even when we face no intervention by God.

Be open-minded, nonjudgmental, and unprejudiced

Mark 1: 1-8 (# 5B)

A race for 1,800 homing pigeons was conducted from Virginia. The pigeons were expected to land in a destination about 200 miles away in Pennsylvania. Except for about 300, the majority landed in places like Delaware, New Jersey, and Oklahoma. In another race, 700 out of 900 missed their targeted course. An interesting study revealed what may have distracted the directional system of the pigeons. Loss of directional flight was attributed to sunspot activity. Theories were proposed postulating that usage of cellular telephones interfered with the instinctive flight orientation of the pigeons. People experience loss of direction and a sense of confusion when the rhythmic pattern of life is confounded by serious illness of themselves or loved ones or a devastating turn of events (Homily Helps, 2002). Despite centuries of prophetic warnings, the people of Israel missed the long-awaited Messiah. Decades after the death and resurrection of Jesus, many Pharisees and scribes continued to deny the Son of God. In fact, no character in Mark's gospel is capable of making such a statement until the end as "Truly this man was the Son of God" by the centurion at the foot of the cross (Mk 15: 39). With all the wonder and amazement there unfolds such a rush of events surrounding the Son of Man that many people so easily miss him by being distracted by their own worlds.

The term "gospel" had not come into usage to mean a written document. In the Roman world a common reference of the word was made to signify tidings with regard to the celebration of the birth rule of the emperor. Mark introduces the word to mean the glad tidings of Jesus the Son of God whose coming marks a startling reality in the history of human beings. The age of the prophets ended 400 years before Christ. Rabbis and scribes customarily examined the laws, the first five books of the Torah, and the prophets to understand their implication for contemporary events. They looked for images and prophecies that might translate current affairs. Mark quotes the words of the prophet in Isaiah 40: 3 in which a messenger announces the second exodus from Babylon into the land of Jerusalem. Combined with that are messages from Malachi 3: 1 where God promises to send a messenger and Exodus 23: 20, where God promises to raise a prophet like Moses. Mark finds fulfillment of those prophecies in

John the Baptist as the messenger and Jesus the divine Son. John preaches a baptism of repentance for the forgiveness of sins (1: 4). Repentance did not just entail merely feeling guilty, ashamed, and fearful, but it demanded a sense of openness to the creative ways of God. The greater the open-mindedness, the greater was the response and acceptance.

From the clothing of John, we find his soul-searching ways of being open to God through the ascetic life. A subtle voice within him prompted him to proclaim the message without being sure who the Messiah was. He seems to have had a vague sense of someone more important than himself, whose sandal strap he was unworthy to stoop and unfasten (1: 7). The Messiah was mightier than he, because John only baptized with water, and he with the Holy Spirit (1: 8). In fact, until John saw Jesus coming out of the water and the Spirit descending upon him, he had no idea who the person was (1: 10). He had to be very open-minded, minute by minute, day by day, to discern God's ways of calling and revealing his "beloved Son" (1: 11).

The vagueness of calling is also experienced in Jesus who aligns himself with sinners. The one who had no sin thought he needed to be baptized. Open-mindedness is coupled with extraordinary humility. The Spirit will drive "him into the desert" to make him conscious of the fact that he indeed is the Son of God who will act as the Son of Man (1: 12). We need to be unbiased and unprejudiced in our ways of evaluating unexplainable events such as losses, grief, and sudden turns of events. That is when we become innocent like children and remain with a sense of wonder. God embraces us always; no matter what happens, there is never abandonment. The ability to trust God in the mysteries of our lives will require an extraordinary faith that will result from a nonjudgmental attitude toward ourselves, events, and others.

Living in the now

John 1: 6-8; 19-28 (# 8B)

In 1835, an Italian psychiatrist received a new patient who suffered from severe depression and anxiety. A thorough physical examination revealed that the patient was in excellent shape. Therefore, the psychiatrist suggested that he immerse himself in laughter and fun. As a good way to start he recommended that the patient go to the new circus in town in which the world-renowned clown Grimaldi was reported by the media as making people laugh uproariously. The depressed patient said to the psychiatrist, "Sir that is impossible." When the therapist asked him why, he said, "Because I am Grimaldi." Grimaldi was faking happiness through laughter, when deep within he suffered terrible depression and anxiety (Homily Helps, 2002). Are we not deceived by our perception or expectation of realities as happy or sad? Our sorrowfulness is as much founded in love as is happiness. An outwardly happy person may not interiorly experience joy. An externally grief-stricken person may experience an inner stability that does not derive from physical or emotional activities. Love resides deep within.

From the questioners such as the Levites, priests, and the Pharisees who addressed themselves to John the Baptist, we learn about their expectations of life. To the priests and Levites who inquired who John was, the Baptist admits that he was not the Christ, the Messiah (Jn 1: 20). Neither did he consider himself Elijah or the Prophet (1: 21). Elijah was expected to return. "Lo, I will send you Elijah, the prophet, before the day of the Lord comes" (Mal 3: 23). "I will raise up for them a prophet like you" in Deuteronomy (18: 18). Religious leaders expected a political Messiah, the anointed one who would free people from Roman bondage and establish an earthly kingdom for Israel. Their expectations about the Messiah centered on great events that characterized the great prophets Moses and Elijah.

Contrary to common expectation, the Baptist simply proclaims the past prophesies and believes that they are being fulfilled in their believing right now. Part of the prophecy relates to him because he believes he is the messenger who is announcing the arrival of the Messiah and is preparing the way of the Lord. Quoting Isaiah (40: 3), the Baptist refers to Jesus as he mentions the word "Lord" (Jn 1: 23). The evangelist John witnessed two developments at the end of the first century. One was concerning a group of believers that was frustrated over the delay of the return of Jesus, his second coming, because they had expected to be raised with him to heaven and were dying without seeing the promise fulfilled.

Second, persecution made the disappointment much more pronounced. Paul's communities experienced similar disappointments. The latter related to the hostile Jews who exposed the Christ believers to life-threatening conditions such as persecution by expelling them from the synagogues. The reason for this was that some did not believe that the one who called himself the Son of God and who performed miracles could have been the Messiah because he was shamefully crucified and died. The Messiah, the liberator, could not have died because he was expected to save everyone. Their influence dissuaded fledgling members from trusting Jesus as the Messiah. His divinity was being questioned, suspected, and denied.

While the persecuted early Christian community eagerly awaited the imminent coming of the Lord, it was tempted to disbelieve Jesus who himself was persecuted and crucified. The evangelist John convinces both groups to recognize that the risen Savior was already powerfully present in their midst. That is why he says, "There is one among you whom you do not recognize" (Jn 1: 26). Those who are poor, homeless, lonely, betrayed, depressed, and persecuted are asked to recognize that they are being made more Christ-like. Others who minister to them are invited to reach out to the Christ in them, respectfully and reverentially and not just out of pity. Even as we expect a better future tomorrow we are called to embrace the "now" in which Christ is present as gloriously as when he ultimately returns.

For nothing will be impossible for God

Luke 1: 26-38 (# 11B)

One evening The Learning Channel (TLC) broadcast an hour-long segment on Progeria, a rare childhood condition. When shocked parents were unable to fathom the stunted growth of their children and sought the advice of physicians, they were devastated to hear how their children were permanently dwarfed and crippled by the disease. Each year the children grew, they advanced seven years in age. By ten, they looked like older adults with no hair on their heads and disfigured with aged teeth and bodies. Surprisingly, the parents who felt sad and angry at God for punishing their children rather than the parents themselves were amazed at how the children accepted their lives no matter how disfigured they may have been. Other gifted humans who came into contact with these children saw them as having a tremendous inner power that they themselves lacked. From the gospel we learn that once we accept anything impossible as God's gift, we gain confidence to journey with God in the unknown.

The annunciation account from Luke and Matthew are believed to have been created in the oral tradition several decades after the birth, death, and resurrection of Jesus. While in Matthew, the Angel Gabriel speaks to Joseph, Luke records him addressing Mary. Luke's account follows the pattern of communication related to the birth of Isaac (Gen 18: 1-15) and Samson (Jgs 13: 2- 7, 24-25a). The Angel's annunciation of the good news is treated with fear by the recipient and the person is subsequently reassured. When a question is raised, a sign is given for the fulfillment of the promise. It is not that Mary earns the honor, but she merely becomes a recipient of God's gift promised to Israel a long time ago. The promise made to King David through the Prophet Nathan is echoed in the words of the Angel to the fearful Mary: "The Lord God will give him the throne of David his father, and he will rule over the house of Jacob forever" (Lk 1: 32-33). Yahweh promised to establish a house for David (2 Sam 7: 11) and make his royal throne firm and endure forever (2 Sam 7: 12, 13, 16). These words were believed by the people of Israel literally. God would abide by the covenant love he promised the people of Israel. Although the Babylonian exile shocked them, they hoped against hope that God would establish a geopolitical freedom by defeating their enemies and remain with them in their earthly kingdom forever. The Angel's words were later understood as God's fulfillment of the promise of a spiritual and eternal kingdom. Therefore, they are theological in that sense.

But the information is also Christological in that it reveals the identity of Jesus as divine Messiah conceived by the power of the Holy Spirit. Mary is bewildered and asks how this is going to be possible since she has had no relations with a man. Mary will conceive by the power of the Holy Spirit, remain a virgin, and bear the Son of the Most High whom she will name Jesus (Lk 1: 31), a mystery that was previously unknown as Paul claims in Romans (16: 25-27). To facilitate her trust in God, a sign is given to her. Her cousin Elizabeth, barren and old, has already conceived and is in her sixth month "for nothing will be impossible for God" (Lk 1: 37). Other questions she may have entertained, such as how she was going to explain herself to her betrothed and her family, remain still as matters unresolved and unanswered. She did not understand but yet believed in her heart. She surrenders to accept the promise without understanding it because she simply trusts God's fulfillment of the promise.

Mary will promise to be God's maid and allow God's will to be done according to God's word. She conceived the Son of God not only biologically but spiritually. Mary becomes a preeminent disciple of Jesus, one who will put his word into practice. "Mary is blessed more by believing than conceiving" says St. Augustine. Conception of God's word can be possible for all those who choose to believe without understanding. To place our faith in God when matters are unclear, unknown, uncertain, unfair, and unjust makes anyone "Mary." Her own son will dare to accept the cross knowing full well its burden, not according to his will but the one in whom he will place all his trust. "Not my will but yours be done" (Lk 22: 42).

God is not at the top but at the bottom

Luke 2: 1-14 (# 14ABC)

Jolie of Croton-on-Hudson was reported in the Westchester daily The Journal News of having celebrated Christmas differently than most people. Responding to a request by the Westchester County Department of Social Service, she budgeted $2,500 towards Christmas presents for teenagers living in foster homes and private residential facilities. Essentially, it meant her family members receive merely a card stating that on their behalf a gift was donated to the needy. She meticulously bought items such as boots, computer games, and jackets worth from $10 to over $100. Her unusual generosity enabled her family to dig deeper into their wallets for her cause. If humanitarianism moved Jolie to act on pity and sympathy, deeper faith would push her to reach out to them respectfully and reverentially as if the children were Christ himself, perhaps much more generously than budgeted. Deep faith also will challenge the needy children to think of themselves not as merely lucky because some donor was generous, but that they are Christ-like even though their family may have been dysfunctional. Instilling in them this kind of faith and trust in God is as or more important than filling them with generosity. Oscar Romero, the Archbishop of El Salvador, shortly before his assassination at the altar, wrote, "Only the poor, the hungry, those who need someone to come on their behalf can celebrate a genuine Christmas. Only poverty of spirit can enable us to experience the abundant joy of God-with-us." Dispossessing as matter-of-fact leads to possession of God.

Luke's infancy narrative begins with the enrollment of the whole world during the rule of the Roman emperor Caesar Augustus and moves the birth of Jesus into the spotlight. In the midst of a great census of the Roman Empire, God enters human history uneventfully. Only emperors were called saviors because they saved people by providing the peace and stability for which people dreamed. Caesar Augustus' long reign was relatively peaceful, so it is known as Pax Romana. Luke adds a spiritual sense of God's active presence among us to the literal understanding of peace as "absence of war." Luke will establish the lineage of Jesus from David through Joseph because God had made such a promise to David: "Your house and your kingdom shall endure forever before me; your throne shall stand firm forever" (2 Sam 7: 16). Prophesies lingered even during the Babylonian captivity: "The spirit of the Lord God is upon me, because the Lord has anointed me; He has sent me to bring glad tidings to the lowly, to heal the brokenhearted, to proclaim liberty to the captives and release to the prisoners" (Is 61: 1). Therefore freedom was understood in the context of political and economic reality. The early Christian community later understood the liberty God promised as freedom from sin. Luke will incorporate Old Testament imagery, early Christian settings, and the end of the first century understanding of Jesus as Christ, Lord, Savior, and Messiah in the words of the angel.

Luke will move Mary and Joseph to Bethlehem, the city of David. The very description of the birth of Jesus is not dramatic because there is no angelic intervention or communication with them at the moment of birth. Jesus is born to poor Mary and Joseph quite unexpectedly and under poor conditions. She wrapped him up in swaddling clothes and laid him in a manger. The manger is a trough to feed the animals. Symbolically, he will be food for humans just as hay is food for the animals. The animals had no problem recognizing the savior. The words "there was no room for them in the inn" (Lk 2: 7) spiritually means humans are more preoccupied with material and physical matters rather than letting God in. Only the announcement of the angel to the shepherds is dramatic. The most significant incident is revealed to the least of people, often despised by orthodox, good people as impure and unobservant of religious rituals. It symbolizes Jesus' ministry to the lowly, the broken hearted, the captives, the marginalized, and the sinners. Human sinfulness cannot prevent God's love nor can human goodness confer God's grace. It is gratuitous. God is not at the top but at the bottom. We need success and control to live our human lives, but God needs our rejection, failure, loss, and alienation to redeem us. Therefore, Jesus chooses to be born in a stable and shows us the way. We gain life by losing it.

Even believers will have to search for God

Matthew 2: 1-12 (# 20ABC)

When a powerful explosion occurred in a West Virginia coal mine, the families of the miners kept vigil in the nearby Baptist Church, anxiously awaiting news of the rescue of the miners trapped inside a mine, filled with carbon monoxide gas. Eventually, when the rescue team reached the area of accident, word came that with the exception of one, the rest were safe. As the family members rejoiced, three hours later the news was reversed: except one, the other twelve had perished. As the news crew interviewed the family members, they vented their anger and disappointment. In particular, one of the women said, "We are believers. Now we don't even know if there is the Lord. A miracle that was supposed to happen was taken away from us" (The Journal News). Her words connote more her anger and shock than transition from believer to unbeliever. Her knowing of the Lord had suddenly experienced an unknowing of the Lord. Conversely, we could speak of knowing in her unknowing. Her deeper search for God just started. There are believers who are in fact unbelievers, if they do not personalize their belief. Similarly, unbelievers who may not belong to any particular religion may truly be believers, if they lived a very holy life by being selfless, compassionate, God fearing, and generous. They are indeed true believers.

The composition of Matthew's gospel occurs three or four decades after the death and resurrection of Jesus Christ. Even as he composes the infancy narrative, his goal is not to portray an exact historical account but provide a theological, Christological perspective. Relating what happened may not have been his objective as much as relating the meaning of the happenings. What was occuring with his fledgling community resonated with what had happened at the time of Jesus Christ. While Jewish Christians left the community because of persecution, the Gentiles embraced Christianity in large numbers. The savior, who was supposed to be the long-expected Messiah, was perceived as failing to save the Jews from the suffering that led to the deaths of believers. Doubts and unanswered questions made them quit their religion and lose faith in the Messiah. Their rejection reminds Matthew of their unwillingness to recognize the newborn infant and the visit of the Magi from the East despite prophecies of this momentous event.

Third Isaiah offers hope to the returning exiles proclaiming, "Nations shall walk by your light, and kings by your shining radiance....For the riches of the sea shall be emptied out before you, the wealth of nations shall be brought to you....All from Sheba shall come bearing gold and frankincense..." (Is 60: 3, 5- 6). Even in their helpless situation, other nations will perceive the presence of Yahweh and will come to them with treasures to rebuild the temple. Matthew uses that imagery to explain to the believers that the hopes of other nations coming to Yahweh have been fulfilled by the birth of Jesus in their midst. The prophecy of the messianic psalm is realized: "The kings of Tarshish and the islands bring tribute, the kings of Arabia and Seba shall offer gifts. May all kings bow before him, all nations serve him" (Ps 72: 10-11). Matthew will include the imagery of an "advancing star" from the book of Numbers. Balak, the king of Moab, afraid of the Israelites, asks Balaam to curse them. Nonetheless, Balaam recognizing Yahweh says, "I see him, though not now; I behold him, though not near: A star shall advance from Jacob, and a staff shall rise from Israel. That shall smite the brows of Moab..." (Num 24: 17). Although the passage contains a promise of the monarchy, Matthew uses the imagery to communicate a deeper understanding of the identity of the eternal king: Jesus Christ. Jesus Christ was born in the most unexpected circumstances for a Messiah. Contrary to the expectations of political, economic, and emotional freedom for Israel, Jesus freed all humanity from the slavery of sin. Difficult circumstances such as persecution, abandonment, loneliness, loss of people, property, relationships, jobs, and opportunities in fact lead us to search for God. In these unfortunate circumstances lies our search for God. No one person or any institution can offer us the true revelation of God fully. The revelation will become personal in our ongoing struggles provided we remain open-minded in our search for God.

Suffering and humiliation will lead to a now-resurrection

John 1: 35-42 (# 66B)

In one of his audio cassette lectures from the series "Great Themes of Paul: Life as Participation," Fr. Richard Rohr, OFM, develops the idea of three force fields necessary for transformation. First is helplessness, an emotional experience of feeling totally incapacitated. Second is crucifixion, a humiliating physical suffering that is unbearable. Third is an experience of the spirit of God, an experience of death and resurrection where one comes out alive after enduring the two previous force fields. It then leads one to total transformation, being unafraid of any suffering. He recognizes this "pain mysticism" propounded by Paul whom he calls a "pain mystic." Such a person cannot wait for another opportunity for humiliation.

For Paul the meaning of the crucified savior and his resurrection is better understood in his own sufferings. He could state unhesitatingly that like Christ, he had been crucified to the world in a metaphorical and real sense. John relates to the crucified savior in his 90s when he recalled what happened to Jesus in his 30s. John's objective is not to paint a historical but Christological Jesus who is actively present in the midst of his persecuted community even as it experienced his seeming absence or delay in his return. Discouraged by God's lack of intervention as the believers suffered persecution, many, particularly Jesus' believers, began to disbelieve the Messiah they had embraced as the savior and instead rejected him. Maybe their faith in the Messiah was wrong because he himself suffered and died. God had not intervened even when his Son suffered and died. Maybe he was not the Son of God. Perhaps he was a son of a man who claimed to be the Son of Man, the glorious one of God. The Messiah should not have died nor should they be suffering and dying because of their faith in him. Suffering contradicted their faith.

John opens his gospel with a prologue introducing a new genesis, a new beginning. His words in the Prologue (Jn 1: 1-18) begin with the beginning of the Bible: "In the beginning was the Word" (Jn 1: 1). Next, the Book of Signs (1: 19-12: 50) will end with the beginning of his second, the Book of Glory (13: 1-20: 31) where understanding of the Messiah becomes much more complete than at the beginning. Actually, John the Evangelist is introducing the end in the beginning. He uses some key phrases and words that reflect the struggles of his community. John the Baptist does not baptize Jesus but sees a dove descend upon him and remain and makes him known as the one who will baptize with the Holy Spirit. "Behold, the Lamb of God" (Jn 1: 36) refers to 1) the paschal lamb (Ex 12: 1-14) that was slain in Egypt on the night of departure, whose blood was smeared on the lintel to save their children from the angel of death who passed over their homes and 2) Isaiah's imagery of a lamb in his Suffering Servant song (53:7), the lamb that went to slaughter, dumb before its shearers. Both images resonate with the bloodshed of the martyrdom of innocent believers and their unjust suffering. John emphasizes that these innocent sufferers are like Christ.

John wants to draw attention to the presence of God in the suffering and death of his beloved Son. Therefore, he will use words such as "stay," which is the same as "remain," that denotes an abiding or lasting, not temporary, presence of the Father in his Son even as he suffered and died (Jn 1: 39). So is the relationship of the disciple with his beloved Christ. John drives home the fact that the resurrected Christ was very much alive in their midst actively participating in their sufferings and deaths. Therefore, if they "come...[they] will see," which means in making a commitment, they will experience his abiding presence and not absence, distance, or indifference (Jn 1: 39). Although Israel expected the Messiah to restore their kingdom, the Messiah instead suffered to redeem Jews and Gentiles from the sin of unbelief, the refusal to believe in the love of God's only Son. Suffering can reveal the extraordinary presence of God provided we surrender to God. "Finding the Messiah" is a life-long transformation which is more pronounced during humiliation and suffering (Jn 1: 41).

Faith is more important than healing

Mark 1: 40-45 (# 78B)

In a renowned oncology hospital in England, a teenage girl was treated for brain cancer. She was accidentally administered radiation seventeen times more than what was required. The chief of the hospital admitted that the incident occurred due to human error and not because of any mechanical problem. Her shaved head revealed rashes due to excessively administered radiation. Along with her parents the girl expressed her fear of the terrible consequences. It is ironic that the very institution that was supposed to cure her cancer only added to her misery (The Journal News). Like the misfortune that befell this girl, terrible injustices are done to innocent people for whom there is no ultimate justification in this world. Without the hope of eternal life none of our human tragedies can fully be remedied. Jesus wants his audience to know that healing is subservient to his preaching. Preaching will demand that the one who prays believe in his word even in irredeemable circumstances.

At one time leprosy was presumed a deadly disease. Any symptom of the disease was treated with careful examination by priests. First, the priest would quarantine a person with suspicious symptoms on the skin for seven days. If the symptoms persisted, another seven days of isolation would continue. After that isolation, prolongation of the problem would lead the priest to conclude that the person is a leper and needs to be isolated from the community completely. Lepers lived in deserted places far removed from human habitation. How any scab or blotch on the skin is to be carefully investigated by priests and how a leper must be isolated from the community and what he is supposed to do while coming upon a healthy human being is clearly delineated in Leviticus (13: 1-8, 45, 46). Such cruel treatment may be due to the fact that a loving God cannot inflict such a terrible disease on human beings whom God loves. Therefore, it was thought that the leper must have done something terrible to deserve it. The leper suffers a great personal loss and his social isolation from family and friends must also be psychologically painful. He is supposed to shout "Unclean, Unclean" twice to ensure that the healthy person listens to his words. Breaking the rules of quarantine, the leper boldly approaches Jesus, kneels down, and begs him to make him clean. In his heart he knows that Jesus will make him clean because he simply believes in him. Had he done anything terrible, Jesus would forgive him unconditionally.

Jesus leans forward and touches him, breaking the law: "Moved with pity, he stretched out his hand, touched him" (Mk 1: 41). The translation of the phrase "moved with pity," according to one source, is Jesus experiencing a "boiling anger that leads to a groan." How can you be so crudely judged as a terrible sinner? How heartbreaking it is for you to experience this trauma. Jesus came to welcome all to his kingdom. No one will remain uninvited, even though we humans think that sinners should be punished and the good be rewarded. Restoring him to full health, Jesus instructs him to abide by the law and show himself to the priest and offer for his cleansing what Moses prescribed as a proof (Mk 1: 44). He is asked not to publicize his healing, but he goes out and proclaims it to the world, breaking Jesus' rule of silence.

Why does Jesus want to avoid publicity? This is a messianic secret; no one understands Jesus until after his suffering, crucifixion, death, and resurrection. The leper's faith is great but incomplete without this understanding. Jesus cannot be taken as a mere miracle worker. According to John the Evangelist, miracles are only signs presenting the breaking in of God's Kingdom through the power of God present in Jesus. Healing tended to be a goal and the end in itself rather than the means. If it were, healed people may or may not have believed in Jesus because he carried his cross to crucifixion, unwilling or unable to perform a miracle for himself. But Jesus believes that his Father is glorified in his suffering and crucifixion, and that he would rise from the dead even after his unjust execution. You do not understand love if you do not suffer. God's love cannot be understood if we do not suffer. The cross is the final door to glory. Faith in God's "love in cross" is more important than physical and emotional recovery. Therefore, Jesus will instruct his disciples and us, "Whoever wishes to come after me must deny himself, take up his cross, and follow me" (Mk 8: 34). Suffering can reveal extraordinary love that otherwise eludes our grasp in joys and pleasures.

Forgiveness is as unconditional as love

Mark 2: 1-12 (# 81B)

The goal of Jesus coming to Earth is to reveal the love of God for humanity. Contrary to human expectation, the approach of God was just the opposite of what humans believed to be the image of God. Contemporaries of Jesus entertained a very stern, severe, and demanding Personhood of God whereas Jesus revealed a compassionate, merciful, and gentle God who longed to forgive humans even without repentance. Therefore, the revelation was scandalous to the righteous who plotted to crucify him. Barclay (2001) refers to the story of Lewis Hind's essays in his commentaries about how Lewis discovered his father's love. Although Lewis admired and revered his father, he was unable to understand his father's strictness. One Sunday morning Lewis was seated next to his father in church and began to nod his head and fall asleep due to exhaustion when he saw his father's hand rise above him. He was afraid that it would strike him. Instead, his father cuddled the boy. It was on that day he discovered his father's love. Jesus came to correct the wrongly perceived image of God.

Mark's story consists of two different parts: healing of the paralytic on one hand and the portrayal of a conflict on the other. Jesus is in Capernaum and the house is flooded with people; even the doorway is blocked (2: 2). Some scribes, perhaps representatives of the Sanhedrin, are sitting in the front row to observe the happenings, find fault, and then report the matter to the authorities above (2: 6). Unable to gain access to Jesus, four men make an opening in the roof and let down a paralytic in front of Jesus. Jesus is amazed at their faith. Unlike other miracles there is no formal inquiry on the part of Jesus with regard to the faith of the sufferer, nor was there any request on the part of the ill person. Both are implied, and their silence speaks volumes. Marveling at the faith of the believers, Jesus uses an unusual formula, "Child, your sins are forgiven" (2: 5). Did Jesus mean that his illness resulted from his terrible sins as was claimed by the Pharisees and the scribes? It appears as though Jesus is agreeing with the contemporary thinking. Would Jesus tell any person he/she is a terrible sinner?

From the perspective of the paralytic, Jesus hints at the spiritual healing that is still required of him. To believe that God is unfailingly ever-present even in the soul of a paralyzed person is the spiritual healing. Physical and emotional healing is meant to lead one to this extraordinary faith in God. The paralytic lacked that kind of faith which is revealed in his earnest desire for a cure. Therefore, he needs to be forgiven for lack of faith. But from the perspective of the Pharisees, Jesus sends a clear message: If you think that humans are suffering because they committed terrible sins, I want you to know that I freely forgive sins. I do not have to be asked to forgive. It was stunning to the Pharisees and the scribes who believed that if they did everything right, God was bound to bless, and, if they did wrong, God was likely to punish them with suffering.

Unconditional forgiveness was unheard of. Besides, here a human being claims the power to grant forgiveness reserved only for God. The message of Christ is that even a miracle cannot convert people. It did not occur to them that a person who heals a paralytic could be none other than God himself. They could not hear that God equally loved both people who did right and those that did wrong. Doing it right does not mean loving God. Righteousness can be impersonal. Whereas Jesus expected a personal relationship, the religious leaders chose to indulge in mechanical observation of laws, feeling entitled to God's Kingdom. They believed that morality was spirituality. Morality is just the start. It should be the result of the love of God.

Therefore, the people who did everything right and did not do anything wrong failed to fathom the love Jesus revealed, while terrible sinners and the afflicted were enamored of the abundance of God's love revealed in Jesus. They knew that God never excluded them from love because of sinfulness. Their imperfections became the means to fall in love with God. Just as God forgave the depressed and anguished people of Israel in Babylonian captivity, "It is I, I, who wipe out, for my own sake, your offenses" (Is 43: 25), God's forgiveness is so unconditional that it has to be believed in and passively accepted more than repented for and earned.

The Kingdom of heaven is in your cross

Mark 1: 12-15 (# 23B)

At the lowest point of his experience with alcoholism William Wilson, who founded Alcoholics Anonymous (AA), had a very powerful religious experience that led to his eventual freedom from alcohol. He claims to have had an encounter with indescribable white light. "Every joy I had known was pale by comparison. The light, the ecstasy—I was conscious of nothing else for a time." When a "wind of spirit...blew right through him," he was declared a "free man." Later he became conscious of a powerful presence in him righting all his wrongs. For the first time in his life, he felt he was loved and he could love in return. He believed "he glimpsed the great beyond" (Borchert, 2005, pp. 167-68). In his story, we find how he had suffered guilt, addiction, and feelings of being unloved when he had bouts with alcoholism. Being exposed to a tremendous love beyond description enabled him to experience something much more fulfilling than addiction. His draw to addiction was in fact a craving for love.

The people of Israel had illusions about the Kingdom of God. In Jewish apocalypse, the Day of the Lord was associated with the judgment of Israel's enemies. It meant the effective reign of God which included not only the absolute obedience of man but God's supreme control over evil. A political Messiah was to usher in an era of the destruction of Israel's enemies. The Kingdom of God was later realized in Christian understanding as the gradual unfolding of God's Kingdom in stages culminating in the Parousia. Like the people of Israel who expected a physical and material kingdom as opposed to the spiritual reality of ultimate union with God and loved ones, modern people look for security guaranteed by God in material matters. That is why Jesus advocated starting that spiritual union now as opposed to awaiting it in heaven. The start of such a reality was promised by God through the prophets. The time of fulfillment was initiated by Jesus. The coming of Jesus brought heaven on earth literally.

Religious leaders of Jesus' time hoped to achieve the kingdom by following the laws perfectly. Exact performance of the law, they believed, entitled them to heaven. Correct and right moral behavior, they interpreted, earned their right. The words of Jesus are in direct contrast to their hope. "Repent, and believe in the gospel" (Mk 1: 15). What is being fulfilled is not what they felt was entitled to them. It was being given to them as a free gift, grace, and gratuity. If they were given the free gift that they did not deserve or earn they were supposed to simply beg for mercy for being made worthy—repentance. Since this was totally the opposite of their expectations, they had to believe in a new reality. The Kingdom emerging with the arrival of Jesus is to be believed in and accepted as a free gift rather than earned through correct moral behavior. By pure faith in the Son, they had to be merely receptive to it.

During baptism, Jesus is declared to be the "beloved Son" by the Father (1: 11). Once he becomes conscious of his status and mission, he is driven into the desert to be tempted by Satan. Jesus sees the path laid by his Father and the options presented by Satan. The command of the Father was to demonstrate the divine love unconditionally even if he ended up on the cross and died. He had faith that his Father would raise him from the dead if he were to die. But Satan tempted him to use his powers—powers equal to that of the Father. He could destroy his enemies and establish the Kingdom. Jesus chose to surrender all his power as a Son equal to his Father. Even though he could have escaped from the humiliation of passion and death on the cross he embraced them fully as a human in his incarnation. Surrendering our lives into God's hands during inexplicable and unavoidable circumstances will require great faith in God. It will mean the letting go of our illusions about our life: That the safer and more secure life is, the more God is present. Even as we suffer we, in fact, participate in God's Kingdom. That is the way Jesus has showed his disciples. Our belief in his words will require whole-hearted open mindedness.

Conclusion

⟶———————————⟵

My heart always desired to know what sustained some humble and illiterate people to remain sustained in prayer for hours. Even though it appeared to be effort-filled for me to imitate their ways, something in me said it must have been a gift for them. Does that mean that some are given the grace to pray wholeheartedly while others are not? Would God be partial in bestowing his gifts? What is it that those individuals did to learn to pray in such a mesmerizing manner? Did they simply exercise some forms of prayer persistently which then accidentally enabled them to be drawn to pray and thereby develop an interior desire?

When I analyzed some of the prayer methods of the mystics as a part of my doctoral research and experimented with some of them myself, they led me to a centering experience that I had never experienced before. It appeared in small increments as I committed to pray following those methods. The more I learned, the more I was eventually drawn to them. Yes, it is a gift but it is an effort-filled one. It is gratuitous and my attempts are only desperate efforts to receive the grace. Initial efforts lead to an effortless condition where you realize that it is completely free and not a result of your initiative. It is also an extraordinary inner focus, making you completely oblivious to the externals.

Another aspect of my learning was that the prayer exercise itself became an experience of love. Often I have prayed intellectually and emotionally for something, but now I pray that it may simply lead to a greater experience of love. Prayer can become an experience of deep love whereby you do not ask for anything because the prayer becomes a reward in itself. It transcends thoughts and feelings and creates a contemplative mind that begins then to view reality differently. It enables one not to think with a calculative mind but rather with heart. It enables me to be comfortable with uncertainty and confusion. You can be satisfied without comprehension and control. You can enter into a state of pure being as opposed to state of doing, performing, earning, or achieving. The state of being and the state of doing merge, and the end result is an encounter with an extraordinary presence. You are present to the unconditional presence of God within. In that state, the word of God is much transformed in its meaning. It is as if the meaning simply comes to you rather your searching for meaning in the sacred word. It comes in small measure, but it is great because it is completely new, exciting, and affirming. It is ever new because the inspiration mesmerizes you. It is different from what the calculative mind offers. It appeals more to the heart than to mind. I hope and pray that you practice these methods, experience the greatest love, and receive God's inspiring message.

References

Amalraj, L. (2002). Imagery's place in physical, psychological, and spiritual healing: Perspectives from religious and mystical traditions. Lewiston, NY: Edwin Mellen Press.

Andrews, L. W. (2005). Stress control: For peace of mind. New York: Barnes & Noble.

Assagioli, R. (1965). Psychosynthesis: A collection of basic writings. New York: Penguin Arkana.

Barclay, W. (2001). The new daily study Bible: The Gospel of Mark. Louisville, London: Westminster John Knox Press.

Barclay, W. (2001). The new daily study Bible: The Gospel of Matthew Vol.2. Louisville, London: Westminster John Knox Press.

Benson, H. (1975). The relaxation response. New York: Avon Books.

Benson, H. (1984). Beyond the relaxation response. New York: Berkley Books.

Benson, H. (1996). Timeless healing: The power and biology of belief. New York: Scribner.

Biema, V., Bjerklie, D., Cullotta, K. A., Park, A., & McDowell, J. (2003, August 3). Just say Om. Time, pp. 49-56.

Borchert, W. G. (2005). The Lois Wilson story: When love is not enough. Center City, MN: Hazelden.

Borysenko, J. (1985). Minding the body, mending the mind (Rev. ed.). New York: Bantam Books.

Borysenko, J. (2007). Minding the body, mending the mind (Rev. ed.). Philadelphia: Da Capo Press.

Caputi, N. (1984). Guide to the unconscious. Birmingham, AL: Religious Education Press.

Chopra, D. (1989). Quantum healing: Exploring the frontiers of mind/body medicine. New York: Bantam Books.

Clement, O. (1995). The roots of Christian mysticism. Hyde Park, NY: New City Press.

Corey, G. (1991). Theory and practice of counseling and psychotherapy (4th. ed.). Pacific

Grove, CA: Brooks/Cole Publishing Company.

Fatula, M. A. (1990). Catherine of Siena's way (Rev. ed.). Collegeville, MN: The Liturgical Press.

Frankl, V. (1975). The unconscious God: Psychotherapy and theology. New York: Simon & Schuster.

Ganss, G. E. (Ed.). (1991). Ignatius of Loyola: Spiritual exercises and selected works. Mahwah, NJ: Paulist Press.

Harkness, G. (1973). Mysticism: Its meaning and message. New York: Abingdon Press.

Hartman, L. F., Skehan, P. W., & Hartdegen, S. J. (Eds.). (1988). The new American Bible. Wichita, KS: Catholic Bible Publishers.

Hughes, B. (2005, November 23). A gift to last a lifetime. The Journal News. pp. A1, A2.

Homily Helps. (2002). Second Sunday of Advent (December 8) [Brochure]. Cincinnati, OH: St. Anthony Messenger Press.

Homily Helps. (2002). Third Sunday of Advent (December 15) [Brochure]. Cincinnati, OH: St. Anthony Messenger Press.

Inge, W. R. (1984). Christian mysticism: Considered in eight lectures delivered before the University of Oxford. London: Methuen & Co., Ltd.

James, W. (1982). The varieties of religious experience. New York: Penguin Books. Johnston, W. (1995). Mystical theology: The science of love. New York: Orbis Books.

Kavanaugh, K., & Larkin, E. E. (1987). John of the Cross: Selected writings. New York: Paulist Press.

Kavanaugh, K., & Rodriguez, O. (1979). Teresa of Avila: The interior castle. New York: Paulist Press.

Kavanaugh, K., & Rodriguez, O. (1979). The collected works of St. John of the Cross (2nd. Ed.). Washington, D. C.: IPS Publications.

Keating, T. (1992). Open mind, open heart: The contemplative dimension of the Gospel. New York: The Continuum Publishing Company.

Keating, T. (1994). Intimacy with God. New York: The Crossroad Publishing Company.

Libreria Editrice Vaticana. (1994). Catechism of the Catholic Church. Liguori, MO: Liguori Publications.

New Revised Standard Version. (1989). The holy Bible. New York: The American Bible Society.

Ornstein, R. (1986). The psychology of consciousness. New York: Penguin Books.

Samuels, M., & Samuels, N. (1975). Seeing with the mind's eye. New York: Random House Inc.

Sanford, J. (1993). Mystical Christianity: A psychological commentary on the Gospel of John. New York: Crossroad.

Schimmel, A. (1975). Mystical dimensions of Islam. Chapel Hill, NC: The University of North Carolina Press.

Smith, H. (1991). The world's religions: Our great wisdom traditions. New York: HarperSanFrancisco.

Underhill, E. (1990). Mysticism: A study in the nature and development of man's spiritual consciousness. London: Methuen & Co., Ltd.

Victoria, N., & David, B. G. (Eds.). (1988). Webster's New World Dictionary of the American English: Third college edition. New York: Simon & Schuster, Inc.

Walsh, J. (Ed.). (1981). The cloud of unknowing. Ramsey, NJ: Paulist Press.

Welch, J. (1982). Spiritual pilgrims: Carl Jung and Teresa of Avila. New York: Paulist Press.

www.ingramcontent.com/pod-product-compliance
Lightning Source LLC
Chambersburg PA
CBHW051528120626
46551CB00012B/1129